Tax Guide 101

# BEING SELF-EMPLOYED

by

Holmes F. Crouch
*Tax Specialist*

Published by

Allyear Tax Guides
**20484 Glen Brae Drive
Saratoga, CA 95070**

**ISBN    0-944817-06-8**

**LCN  92-73880**

**Printed  in  U.S.A.**

---

**Series  100**
### Individuals  and  Families

---

Tax Guide 101

**BEING  SELF-EMPLOYED**

---

*For other titles in print, see page 224.*

*The author*: **Holmes F. Crouch**
*For more about the author, see page 221.*

# PREFACE

If you are a **taxpayer** whose income exceeds $40,000 per year, this book can be helpful to you. It is designed to be read — from cover to cover — in less than six hours. Or, you can skim read it in approximately 30 minutes.

Either way, you are treated to **tax knowledge** . . . *beyond the ordinary*. The "beyond" is that which you cannot find in official instructions, and that which is not ordinarily imparted to you by professional counselors.

Taxpayers have different levels of interest in a selected tax subject. For this reason, this book starts with introductory fundamentals and progresses through some rather complex situations. You can verify the progression by chapter and section in the table of contents. In the text, "applicable law" is quoted in pertinent part. Key interpretive phrases and key tax forms are emphasized. Real-life examples are given . . . in down-to-earth style.

This book has 12 chapters. This number provides depth without cross-subject rambling. Each chapter starts with a head summary of meaningful information.

To overcome the humdrum of ordinary tax jargon, informative diagrams and tables are placed strategically throughout the text. Most of the illustrations are true originals. By leafing through page by page, reading the summaries and section headings, and glancing at the diagrams and tables, you can get a good handle on the matters covered.

Effort has been made to update and incorporate all of the latest tax law changes that are significant to the title subject. However, "beyond the ordinary" does not encompass every conceivable variant of fact and law that might give rise to protracted dispute and litigation. Consequently, if a particular statement or paragraph is crucial to your own specific case, you are urged to seek professional counseling. Otherwise, the information presented is general and is designed for a broad range of reader interests.

*The Author*

# INTRODUCTION

Becoming and staying self-employed is an attribute of self-discipline and self-survival. It is a form of occupation where titles and wages are unimportant. Instead, the primary rewards are self-accomplishment and inner satisfaction. These are the realizations of dreams. Creative humans like to be financially independent; be in business for themselves; and be "their own boss."

Rarely do self-employment activities produce great wealth. But said activities can — and do — produce a great peace of mind which wealth alone cannot provide.

By being self-employed, we mean a taxpayer who is not regularly classed as an employee or as a statutory employee. He/she is an **independent contractor** engaging in a trade or business in sole proprietorship form. The products or services offered to the general public — the variants of which we'll discuss herein — are presented so, on a continuous and ongoing basis.

A self-employed person is distinguished from other forms of occupation in that one pays a **second** income tax called: *self-employment tax*. This is a combined social security tax and medicare tax. It is the one combined tax that is guaranteed to increase over the years, and from which reduced benefits will be derived.

In many cases, particularly in the early years of self-employment, the second tax on income is greater than the first tax (the regular income tax) on the same income. Both taxes apply to the net earnings from self-employment. The difference is that there are *no offsets* against the second tax, as there are against the first tax.

The two differing income taxes mean that two separate tax schedules must be attached to your annual Form 1040: U.S. Individual Income Tax Return. The first of the two taxes derives from Schedule C (Form 1040): **Profit or Loss From Business**; the second tax derives from Schedule SE: **Self-Employment Tax**. Explaining these two schedules — and the backup information needed for them — is what this book is all about.

We want you, as a self-employed individual, to understand the workings of these two tax schedules, and how you can use them to your best benefit. Your "best benefit," of course lies in your minimizing the two taxes and in maximizing the satisfaction from your chosen trade or business.

Whether you are single, married, divorced, remarried, widowed, with or without dependent children or parents, the above two schedules — C and SE — stand apart from all other tax matters on your annual Form 1040. If you are married, and both you and your spouse are self-employed, a Schedule C and a Schedule SE are required for you, and an entirely separate Schedule C and Schedule SE are required for your spouse. This is so, regardless of whether you file married jointly or married separately.

There is one predominant, ever watchful, adversary (enemy) of every self-employed individual. Said adversary is *government*: federal government, state government, and local government. For some reason, government at all levels takes particular aim at self-employeds. Government does this with punitive intent and restrictive measures. Agencies such as the Internal Revenue Service (IRS), for example, just love to give self-employeds a "hard time."

One reason for government giving self-employeds a hard time may arise from the phenomenon known as "professional jealousy." Many government employees, like all other humans, would like to be their own boss . . . but they can't. They need the security and benefits of being on the public payroll. As a result, they harbor an inner dislike for those who are independent of government.

There is a more probable reason for the adversarial stance of government towards self-employeds. Said individuals comprise a vast sea of small business doers who are easier to tax pluck than those corporate Goliaths of society. It is simply so much easier for the IRS, for example, to pick on the little guy. Consequently, towards the end of this book we'll tell you about the **audit strike** that will inevitably come your way.

Within five to ten years after becoming self-employed, we can virtually guarantee that the IRS will be after you with fang and tong. That agency dislikes self-employed taxpayers with a passion. Unless you are prepared for this, you will not last long as a self-employed.

If you get nothing else out of this book, we think we can help prepare you for surviving any and all shark attacks from the IRS. If so prepared, you can count on being self-employed into retirement age . . . and beyond.

# CONTENTS

# 1

# GENERAL REQUIREMENTS

> Independent Thinkers And Doers Who Are Self-Reliant Comprise The Best Candidates For Self-Employment. Also Required Are Years Of Preparatory Experience With Various Employers Issuing W-2's. Self-Discipline Towards Your Own Tax Returns (Forms 1040, Etc.) Is A Good Indicator Of Solo Business Success Where Tax Matters Often Dominate. Other Qualifications Include Habits of Saving And Investing, Attitude Towards Insurance Risks, Awareness Of Lawsuits, Fair Treatment Of Customers, And the Active Participation And Ongoing Support Of Your Spouse.

Before becoming self-employed, one needs to develop adequate knowledge, expertise, and experience in some endeavor with respect to the marketability of a product, service, or talent. Rarely does one complete his education with the expectation of launching immediately into full-time self-employment. There needs to be some "testing of the waters," before swimming off on one's own.

In most situations, self-employment is not a preplanned goal. More often than not, it is something that one *evolves into*. That is, he/she has some prior experience with one or more employers, and a situation arises which either voluntarily or involuntarily directs one out on his own. Sometimes, it's almost a situation where one has no other choice. This need not be bad.

The key ingredient to successful self-employment is self-reliance . . . in some endeavor. Achieving this self-reliance rarely comes about before age 35; it may even extend to age 50. The reason for this maturational delay is the need for build-up time to gather financial resources, occupational competency, and a customer/client base.

Therefore, in this introductory chapter, we want to lay the foundation for your understanding of why self-reliant character is so important to self-employment. This foundation is the process of discovering within yourself your strengths and weaknesses, and your determination to succeed. You need sufficient occupational time with one or more employers for discovering yourself. Once you have left the paycheck comfort of employment, you are out in the cold strictly on your own.

## Workplace Human Types

In the many workplaces of the U.S. (and the world), there are three basic types of human beings. There are (1) the leaders, (2) the followers, and (3) the independents.

The leaders are the movers and shakers of the world. Their driving motivations are power and wealth. Regardless of the organizational structure in which they operate — corporate, military, government, religious, or international — leaders rise to the top by virtue of their great energy, intelligence, and activational wheelings and dealings.

But leaders are not self-reliant. They need followers; they need staff assistants; and they need an organizational structure within which they can climb. They need followers whom they can direct and check up on. They need assistants on whom they rely, and on whom they can pin the blame when things go wrong. They need an organizational structure for consolidating power at each upward rung, and for the rewards of wealth, privileges, and perks. Leaders are not good candidates for self-employment for the simple reason that they have absolutely no interest in becoming so.

Followers are not self-reliant either. Followers need leaders. Followers are those who produce the products and furnish the services which their leaders instruct them to do. Followers also need structural rungs for grading their performance and worth in wages, salaries, and other forms of compensation. Followers are those who need a steady paycheck, enjoy fringe benefits, and who look forward to their employer-paid times-off for vacations.

Followers rarely become successful self-employeds. This is because of their dependency on the regularity of paychecks and benefits. They are not sufficiently self-reliant to weather financial storms and dry spells of self-employment. When unemployed, they may be forced into trying a hand at self-employment. But the moment an employment opportunity comes along, they immediately abandon their self-employment endeavor.

Independents, on the other hand, are neither leaders nor followers. In certain respects, they are misfits in the workplace. They are highly capable and self-motivated persons who, it seems, just can't find their place in structural organizations. At times, they may serve as temporary leaders or as substitute followers. But in leadership roles they come to realize that they don't have the charisma or the stomach for intrigue that haloes those loving power. In followership roles, they tend to be unhappy; they continually question the competence, direction, and goals of their leaders. They become obsessed with the belief that they can do things better, more efficiently, and for less cost. Without realizing it, these are the very traits for successful self-employment.

Occupational independents are that way because, instinctively, they think independently and they do their own thing independently. They need very little leadership, and they can tolerate only a limited amount of followership. They are competent, knowledgeable, and self-reliant. Because of underlying financial needs, they seldom realize that self-employment is their true destiny for occupational fulfillment.

As a useful summary of the above, we present Figure 1.1. The features presented are broad generalizations of the likelihood of your becoming self-employed.

### Employee Experience Essential

Once you become self-employed, you must perform as a "one man show" (or one woman show). You're the leader, the follower, the doer, the thinker, the designer, the producer, the promoter, the buyer, the seller, the marketer, the advertiser, the biller, the collector . . . and whatever else needs to be done in your prospective self-endeavor.

But before you can do all of these things acceptably, you need hands-on employment experience with — preferably — several employers. When with a large structured organization, you need to acquire rounded experience in several different divisions or departments. You want to engage in a variety of different nonroutine tasks. If employed with a medium-sized semi-structured entity, you need to experience different task assignments at each

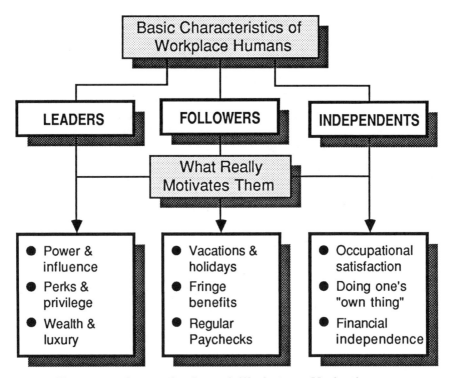

**Fig. 1.1 - Generalization of Workplace Motivations**

organization. If employed with multiple small, nonstructured enterprises, you need experience in performing double- or triple-tasks simultaneously. That is, you wear two (or three) hats, so to speak.

If, in the entity where you are employed, you are not directly assigned to a particular task (or tasks) essential to broadening your experience, cultivate friendship with others who are performing the task(s). By talking with them and asking questions, you can learn much that will come in handy later.

Ideally, experience over several years as a self-motivated employee should provide direct and/or indirect exposure to every function of the entity that is applicable to your educational background and natural aptitudes. The idea is to become knowledgeable in as many facets of your employer's activities as possible. You want to find out what he does right and what he does wrong.  What special niches in the market place is he successful in?  In what areas is he not so successful?

If you can, you'd like to find out about your  employer's advertising, marketing, billing, and collection practices.  You must not be intrusive.  You simply want to be aware of the uncertainties and disappointments — and of the competition — that your employer experiences.  These are the kinds of matters that you, too, will have to face, once you become self-employed.

### Ever  Examine  a  W-2?

If you've been employed for a number of years, you surely must know what a W-2 is.  But have you ever examined it closely?  Have you ever looked at all the boxes thereon and wondered what they are all about?  If you have, you probably appreciate your employer a lot more.  He's done much accounting to the government (federal, state, local) for you.

Just in case you haven't examined a W-2 lately, we present its complete format in Figure 1.2.  Note immediately its title: **Form W-2 Wage and Tax Statement** (year), Department of Treasury, Internal Revenue Service.  Also note the number of information boxes — 29 in all!

We show in Figure 1.2 Copy C:  For  EMPLOYEE'S RECORDS.  There is also a Copy A:  For Social Security Administration; a Copy B:  To Be Filed With Employee's FEDERAL Tax Return; a Copy 1:  To Be Filed With Employee's State, City, or Local Income Tax Return; a Copy 2: For State, City, or Local Tax Department; and a Copy D:  For Employer.  Altogether, there are six copies of the W-2 which have to be prepared, filed, and punched into some government agency's computer data base.

We call your attention to the headnote in Figure 1.2 which reads—

*This information is being furnished to the Internal Revenue Service.  If you are required to file a tax return, a negligence penalty or other sanction may be imposed on you if this income is taxable and you fail to report it.*

When you turn Copy C of Form W-2 over, you'll find 10 paragraphs of instructions thereon.  Have you ever read *any* of these

| Form W-2 Wage and Tax Statement | | Year_____ | |
|---|---|---|---|
| 1 Control number | This information is being furnished to the Internal Revenue Service. If you are required to file a tax return, a negligence penalty or other sanction may be imposed on you if this income is taxable and you fail to report it. | | |
| 2 EMPLOYER'S name, address, and ZIP code | 6 Pension Plans, etc. ☐ ☐ ☐ ☐ ☐ ☐ ☐ | | |
| | 7 Allocated Tips | 8 Advance EIC payment | |
| 3 EMPLOYER'S Identification No. | 9 Federal income tax withheld | 10 Wages, tips, other compensation | |
| 4 EMPLOYER'S State I.D. No. | 11 Social security tax withheld | 12 Social security wages | |
| 5 EMPLOYEE'S Social Security No. | 13 Social security tips | 14 Medicare wages and tips | |
| 19 EMPLOYEE'S name, address, and ZIP code | 15 Medicare tax withheld | 16 Nonqualified plans | |
| | 17 See Instrs. on back | 18 Other | |
| 20 ///////// | | | |
| 21 ///////// | 22 Dependent care benefits | 23 Benefits incl. in Box 10 | |
| 24 State income tax | 25 State wages, tips, etc. | 26 Name of state | |
| 27 Local income tax | 28 Local wages, tips, etc. | 29 Name of locality | |

Fig. 1.2 - Complete Format; Annual Wage and Tax Statement

instructions? The heading is: Notice to Employee, followed by paragraphic subheadings as—

- Getting a Refund
- Earned Income Credit
- Making Corrections
- Credit for Excess Social Security Tax
- Box 6 — Pension plans, etc.
- Box 7 — Allocated tips
- Box 16 — Nonqualified plans

- Box 17 — Codes A to N
- Box 22 — Dependent care benefits
- Box 23 — Fringe benefits

Box 17: Codes A to N, says—

*If there is an amount in Box 17, there should be a code (letter) next to it. You need this information to complete your tax return. The codes are:*

A — Uncollected social security tax on tips
B — Uncollected medicare tax on tips
C — Cost of group life insurance over $50,000
D — Section 401(k) contributions
E — Section 403(b) contributions
F — Section 408(k)(6) contributions
G — Section 457 contributions
H — Section 501(c)(18)(D) contributions
J — Nontaxable sick pay
K — Excess golden parachute tax
L — Nontaxable expense reimbursement
M — Uncollected social security tax on C (above)
N — Uncollected medicare tax on C (above)

All of the above information, which is applicable to you as an employee, has to be accounted for and filled in by your employer. Would you not agree that doing so is a formidable task?

If you were to become self-employed and had your own employees, who do you think would have to do all of the W-2 accounting?

YOU, of course.

If this prospect frightens you, or if you have not given the W-2 serious thought, perhaps self-employment is not your cup of tea.

## Consistent, Timely Tax Returns

One of the most character-revealing activities of occupational (income-producing) life is a person's own Form 1040 tax return. If you truly dread the annual ritual of filing an income tax return — that is, you put off and put off doing it — you have already revealed a side of your character which will **not** stand you well in self-employment.

More than any other single accounting activity of adulthood, your attitude towards your own tax return reveals a lot. If you file on time, year after year, and do so in a competent and diligent way, you have exhibited a natural and inherent self-discipline. This is the very kind of character needed to "challenge the system" and not let it beat you down. Taxation in our society is a deliberate attempt to beat you down at every entrepreneurial step of the way. You can't let this happen.

There are income taxes, excise taxes, sales taxes, property taxes, gift taxes, inheritance taxes, social security taxes, medicare taxes, pension taxes, penalty taxes, employer taxes, self-employment taxes . . . and on and on. You cannot escape these taxes when self-employed. Taxation is the source for feeding what appears to be the BIG BLACK HOLE of government. Not all taxes are bad: only those which are used for flaky projects — local, national, international — which benefit special interest groups.

Self-discipline in meeting all tax challenges head on is an important ingredient to successful self-employment.

You cannot escape taxes . . . and you shouldn't try. Taxes are a surcharge for the air you breathe. To survive as a human being you must have air; to survive in self-employment you must face the onerous and distractive role of taxation. If you habitually get behind in tax matters, you are rapidly digging your own grave.

Many — probably most — new businesses fail because the owners thereof become lethargic and antipathetic towards the timely filing of various tax returns. You don't have to love paying taxes to succeed. You simply have to accept the burden; try to minimize all taxes that you can; and discipline yourself to "get them out of the way." You do want to get on to more self-fulfilling endeavors, don't you?

## Savings and Investments

There is another self-reliant characteristic that you should develop during your years of employment with one or more employers. It is the habit of saving money and, when appropriate, investing some. By "savings," we mean habitually (and regularly) putting some of your take-home pay aside. Then when you have accumulated a cushion amount, you begin a modest investment program that offers reasonable expectation of growth.

If you haven't already done so, you should start saving at least 10% of your take-home pay, each pay period. Yes, we know; this is easier said than done. But, unless you develop the will power and determination to save, you'll never be in a position to launch successfully into self-employment. You've got to grit your teeth, knuckle down, and demonstrate — to yourself, if to no one else — that you have the capacity to save 10% or so. Do this for at least three years. By the end of this time, the habit should become more or less routine. Some employers, through company-sponsored savings plans, offer specific incentives and encouragement for establishing your savings goals.

Once the 10% savings habit has become entrenched, your next challenge is to up the ante to 20%. The additional 10% is for commencing a modest investment program. Growth funds of the no-load mutual fund type are the ideal way to start doing this. You can select among various degrees of growth orientation to meet your own philosophical bent. Be prudent. Do *not* invest your core savings; invest only the excess over your core savings.

Why is all of this so important? There are two reasons.

One, for any self-employment endeavor you will need "front money" to start your own business. At the very minimum, you'll need to put up some money for business cards, letterhead, small tools, and a telephone. For startup purposes, it is far better to cash in on your own investments than to rely on borrowing from family and friends. Unless you have significant equity in a home or other property, no bank is going to lend money to a newly self-employed person for startup.

Two, rarely does any self-employment endeavor produce a steady stream of income throughout the year. There are good seasons, low seasons, and off seasons. Every small business experiences cyclic periods of income — and no income — as we depict in Figure 1.3. Consequently, one always needs a little cushion to carry him over the rough spots and low seasons. As a rule of thumb, you should have enough cushion money of your own to carry you for at least six months. A full year's cushion money (from your own savings and investments) would be better.

### Calculated Risks and Insurance

How do you feel about insurance? Are you uncomfortable with less than maximum coverage on all insurance-type matters: life, health, dental, disability, accident, car, home, malpractice, unemployment, etc.? Do you try to insure against every

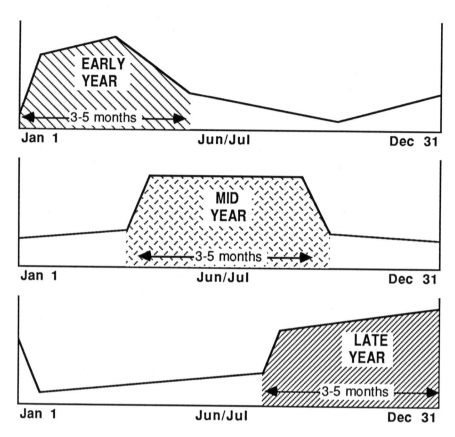

**Fig. 1.3 - Likely "Income Profile" of Self-Employment**

contingency in life? If you do, we don't know how you can be successfully self-employed.

In addition to taxes, insurance premiums and policies can weigh you down and keep you from getting ahead. Furthermore, only limited types of insurance — those related directly to your business — provide any tax benefits.

The point that we are getting at is that all self-businesses involve risks. If your philosophy is to have insurance against every conceivable mishap in life, you'll be too conservative — and too insurance poor — to develop the product, service, expertise, or clientele that you need for self-employment fulfillment. Except for term life, catastrophic insurance, and government-mandated coverage, most people lose money on insurance matters over the long haul. When the chips are down and the claims are in, the "fine print" in many policies and warranties rule out all compassion.

All forms of business life involve calculated risks. You will win some, lose some, and draw some. If you are prone to too much reliance on insurance, it signifies that you are innately risk adverse. We are not advocating imprudence; we're just saying that risk tolerance is another general requirement for self-employment.

## Awareness of Lawsuits

The United States is the most litigious society in the world. On a population per capita basis, we have 20 times more attorneys than other industrial nations, such as Germany and Japan. Sooner or later, anyone in business for himself is hit with a lawsuit. Winning or losing is not a matter of fairness and justice; it is solely a matter of legal *theory* in an adversarial context. This, and the endless fees, is why the legal profession is not held in high regard by the general public.

At best, the legal profession is a "necessary evil" in those situations where bona fide injury has occurred. Although most people are decent, there is always someone who will allege that he or she has been injured in a business transaction with you. Indeed, this may well be the case. If so, and it is alleged that you are responsible, you will have to deal with the matter as amicably as you can. If you cannot do so amicably, be prepared for a lawsuit.

Lawsuits are not only time consuming and distractive, they can drain you emotionally and financially. And they can drive you into a state of cynicism towards all people, attorneys and nonattorneys alike. This is the down side of lawsuits.

There is — believe it or not — a constructive upside to lawsuits. They can sharpen your focus in prejudging the character of your customers, clients, agents, and suppliers. You will learn the hard way how to select those with whom you want to do business, and ferret out those with whom you do not want to do business. The experience of at least one lawsuit in which you are the defendant will probably benefit you more than you may realize. It will make you acutely aware of the legal risks in self-employment. It will induce you to *try* to settle valid complaints without legal proceedings. On the other hand, experience as a defendant will enable you to stand your ground in the face of meritless complaints.

In self-employment as in any other form of business, you need to develop skills and insight for prediagnosing those situations which might give rise to legal repercussions. But no matter how skillful you may become, there will be some person or entity whose intentions will confound you. In this country, there is always someone who wants to sue. These are the risks of every business.

## Treatment of Customers

Contrary to the old adage "the customer is always right," the customer is *not* always right. Customers ignore precautionary warnings; they forget the instructions that are given; they disregard any price breaks that may have been allowed; and they seek to blame the business owner for all the faults and mishaps that occur to a product or service sold/rendered to them. They're just being human. And this is the way you want to treat them: as ordinary humans trying to get the most for their money that they can.

In a self-employed business, a satisfied customer is your ongoing word-of-mouth advertiser. Once you realize this, you will try harder to cultivate your customer base to cause it to grow and expand. One of the best ways for doing this is to treat every customer who has a comment or complaint as though he may be right. If there is reasonable doubt in your mind, give the customer the benefit of that doubt. Giving the customer the benefit of reasonable doubt really works wonders. Most customers have good memories when treated decently.

Giving the benefit of doubt is so unlike that of government taxing agencies. A tax agency such as the IRS, for example, never gives the benefit of doubt. The IRS's position is: "We are right; you have to prove us wrong. We have the power to say 'No' to everything you want to do."

Do you ever wonder why the IRS is so disliked — and distrusted — by the majority of the taxpaying public? Could it be that it never gives its "customers" the benefit of reasonable doubt?

If you treat customers the way the IRS treats taxpayers, you won't last in self-employment one year. Your meanness towards them will spread like wildfire.

Government officials, attorneys, doctors, and accountants often intimidate their clientele rather than cultivate them. They do this unwittingly perhaps, with their "holier than thou" attitude when flaunting their knowledge and prestige. High-priced professionals tend to think that the world owes them a luxurious living, and that the role of their customer base is to support their extravagant lifestyle. If you have been treated this way, you know first-hand what *not* to do.

Most consumers are trying to earn a living and make ends meet. In this process, they want to be treated humanely. This means that as a self-employed, you must discipline yourself against any temptation to gouge or short-change your customers. While some customers may attempt to gouge or short-change you, only a certain few will do so.

Most customers, perhaps 98% or so, respond in kind. That is, you treat them right; they'll treat you right. If you do not believe this, you probably are not destined for self-employment success.

## Importance of Spousal Support

In most self-employed businesses, one's customer base is generally a mixture of men and women. Some will be single persons; many will be married persons; and some will be divorced or widowed. Some will have children, parents, brothers, sisters, uncles, aunts, etc. Because of the mixed marital family status of your customers, you will find it quite beneficial if your spouse (assuming you are married) participates to some degree in your everyday business affairs.

Most successful self-employment businesses start off with strong spousal support. The nonentrepreneurial spouse not only supports the self-employment idea in principle, but also supports it with a participating hand as needed. The nonentrepreneurial spouse may also demonstrate such support by seeking employment — or staying employed — to provide financial backup to the entrepreneurial spouse's business. Until the self-employed business becomes truly self-sustaining, spousal financial backup is indeed needed. An employed spouse who undertakes this role knowingly provides one of the best assurances of ultimate self-employment success.

It seems that customers like knowing that the small business owner's spouse is behind him or her all along the way. This makes customers feel that the business — its product, service, or talent — is likely to be there when the customer needs it. Nothing is more dissatisfying to a customer than dealing with a business owner who is in business one day, and out of business the next. Spousal support that is made obvious to customers tends to imply that the business will be continuous and ongoing.

Should the business grow and prosper, the employed supporting spouse may find it advantageous to cease her or his employment, and participate more directly in business with the entrepreneurial spouse. When this happens, the entrepreneurial spouse can focus more of his/her attention on that which he/she does best. The non-entrepreneurial spouse then takes on a more active supporting role that enables the business to flourish even more.

So important is the role of spousal support that we depict its beneficial features in Figure 1.4. As we have tried to illustrate, a self-employment business with two actively-participating spouses provides better "balance" and better division of tasks. Both spouses are enabled equal opportunity to achieve their own self-fulfillment in the business domain. Married persons who get along well in business, generally get along well in marriage. This makes for more stable and successful self-employment.

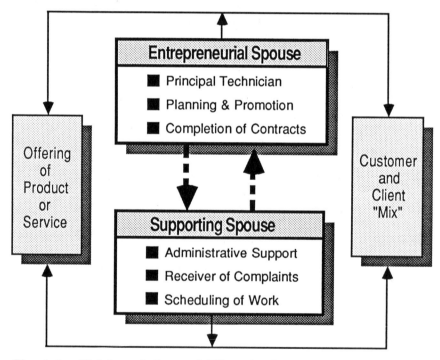

Fig. 1.4 - Division of Spousal Effort in Ongoing Self-Employment

# 2

# HOW TAX DEFINED

Chapter 2 Of The IR Code Is Titled: "Tax On Self-Employment Income." This No. 2 Tax Is Comprised Of Two Parts, Namely: Old-Age Insurance [Sec. 1401(a)] And Hospital Insurance [Sec. 1401(b)]. This Insurance Tax Applies To The NET EARNINGS (Gross Income Less Deductions Allowed) Of Each Self-Employed Individual Engaged In A Trade Or Business For His/Her Livelihood. Where Husband And Wife Are Engaged In The Same Business, Each Spouse Pays His/Her Own Separate No. 2 Tax. The Same Applies To Members Of A General Partnership. Section 1403 Defines The No. 2 Tax As "Contributions," But This Is Misleading.

The Internal Revenue Code devotes three sections (1401, 1402, and 1403) to defining what self-employment is. The tax-defining thrust focuses exclusively on the *second* tax on the net income generated from self-employment.

The second tax on self-employment income is comprised of two parts: (a) social security tax, and (b) medicare tax. We combine these two to call them the *social tax* on self-employed individuals. The idea behind this social tax, allegedly, is for government to "take care of" self-employed individuals in their waning years of retirement, old age, and disability. Government, it seems, declares that it — and only it — has the right to "protect one" in his waning years and, therefore, compulsory social taxes must be imposed.

A truly self-reliant, self-employed person is quite capable of taking care of himself/herself in old age and retirement. But self-reliance by individuals is not something that government mentality understands. An individual who saves, invests, and prepares prudently for his own old age is the target of scorn and punishment by Congress, by IRS officials, by court judges, and by U.S. attorneys. Anyone who dares to side-step the second tax with alternate, equivalent, self-directed programs will experience first-hand how the **power to tax** can be crammed down his throat.

Thus, in this chapter, we want to present the IRS's definition of self-employment, and point out how this second tax destroys the true independence of self-employed persons. We will also point out that there are very few exceptions to, and offsets against, the second tax. For some reason, Congress and the President are unwilling to recognize that by permitting alternatives to the second tax, self-employed individuals could spearhead a whole new era of competitiveness and efficiency in the United States.

## Section 1401 Overview

Chapter 1 of the Internal Revenue Code is titled: *Normal Taxes and Surtaxes*. This is Tax No. 1: the regular income tax. Everyone pays this tax, as they should.

Chapter 2 of the tax code is titled: *Tax on Self-Employment Income*. This is Tax No. 2: social security and medicare. The social security tax is more specifically designated as: *Old-Age, Survivors, and Disability Insurance* [Sec. 1401(a)]. The medicare tax is designated as: *Hospital Insurance* [Sec. 1402(b)]. If these two sub-items are truly "insurance," why are they designated as a tax?

Whenever there is a federal tax — be it No. 1 or No. 2 — there has to be a prescribed tax rate. Sure enough, Section 1401 is titled: *Rate of Tax*. Let us examine what the No. 2 tax rate is.

Subsection 1401(a) reads in essential part as—

*In addition to other taxes, there shall be imposed for each taxable year, on the self-employment income of every individual, a tax equal to . . . 12.40 percent . . . of the amount of the self-employment income for such taxable year.* [Emphasis added.]

Similarly, subsection 1402(a) reads—

*In addition to the tax imposed by the preceding section, there shall be imposed for each taxable year, on the self-employment income of every individual, a tax equal to . . . 2.90 percent . . . of the amount of the self-employment income for such taxable year.*

You add these two Section 1401 tax rates together, and what do you come up with?

Answer: 15.3% (12.40 + 2.90 = 15.3).

Remember, though, the 15.3% is **in addition to** your regular tax rate (Tax No. 1) which may be 28% or so.

Tax No. 2 was first imposed on self-employed individuals in 1954. Its launching rate then was just 3%. That rate produced a self-employment tax of *less than* $100 per year. Today, at a 15.3% rate, the same No. 2 tax can now *exceed* $10,000!

How long will Tax No. 2 stay at 15.3%? No one really knows, but it is probably at or near the tolerance limit for law-abiding citizens.

## Section 1402 Overview

Section 1402 is titled: *Definitions* (plural).

In a domain where the power to tax is tossed around, nothing is simple. Ordinarily, one would think that the term "self-employed" is self-explanatory. It is not. It takes eleven — yes, eleven — subsections to Section 1402 to define that income to which the No. 2 tax applies.

For introductory purposes, the eleven subsections defining self-employment income are:

(a) Net earnings from self-employment.
(b) Self-employment income.
(c) Trade or business.
(d) Employee and wages.
(e) Ministers, members of religious orders, and Christian Science practitioners.
(f) Partner's taxable year ending as a result of death.
(g) Members of certain religious faiths.
(h) Regular basis.
(i) Special rules for options and commodities dealers.
(j) Special rules for certain church employee income.
(k) Applicable contribution base.

Obviously, for space reasons, we cannot quote each of these eleven definitional sections in full.  But we do intend to highlight the key elements of being self-employed for which the No. 2 tax applies.

For example, subsection 1402(h): Regular Basis, is particularly instructive.  It sets forth a three-consecutive-year period for which one is treated as being self-employed "on a regular basis."  One- or two-year nonconsecutive stints do not qualify one as being self-employed.

The precise wording in definition (h) is—

*An individual shall be deemed to be self-employed on a regular basis in a taxable year, . . . if he had net earnings from self-employment, . . . of not less than $400 in at least two of the three consecutive taxable years immediately preceding such taxable year from trades or businesses carried on by such individual.*

Three pertinent points "pop out" of the definitional law, namely:

**One.**  It is the *net* earnings from self-employment to which the No. 2 tax attaches:  NOT the gross income.

**Two.**  The amount of net earnings to which the No. 2 tax attaches is $400 or more in any taxable year.

**Three.**  There can be one loss year, or one year where the net earnings are less than $400 (in any three-consecutive-year period), without losing one's classification as being self-employed.

## "Net Earnings" Defined

Section 1402(a) painstakingly defines the term:  "net earnings from self-employment."  However, the definition is approximately 2,220 words in length.  It addresses the earnings from sole proprietorships, general partnerships, ministers and religious practitioners, Indian tribes, commodities dealers, foreign source income, and community property matters between husband and wife.

For simplification reasons, we'll focus the definition initially on sole proprietorship.  A *sole proprietorship* is a one person (man or woman) trade or business conducted wholly within the United States. Later, we'll address husband and wife businesses, partnerships, and members of religious faiths.

In excerpted form, Section 1402(a) addresses a sole proprietorship as follows—

> *The term "net earnings from self-employment" means the **gross income** derived by an individual from any trade or business carried on by such individual, **less the deductions allowed** by this subtitle* [Income Taxes] *which are attributable to such trade or business.*

In essence, then, the net earnings from self-employment is your gross income less the deductions allowed . . . which are attributable to your trade or business.

In other words, there must be some "gross income" attributable to your trade or business, for which there are some "deductions allowed." Furthermore, the income and deductions must be attributable to the **same** trade or business. That is, you cannot mix several unrelated trades or businesses (such as simultaneously being an employee, investor, or agent) and net them for No. 2 tax purposes. Each trade or business must stand on its own. And for each such business there can be only one owner (except for partnerships which we'll come to later).

As with all tax definitions, the minute we define one term we have to immediately define the related terms. The related terms here requiring definition are: "gross income," "deductions allowed," and "trade or business." These terms are not as self-explanatory as you might hastily conclude.

Except for certain religious persons, the only way to reduce the No. 2 tax on self-employment income is to reduce your net earnings. But the IRS is not going to let you do this at will. It imposes certain restrictions and limitations which enable it to assess the highest possible No. 2 tax. The No. 2 tax combines with revenues from the No. 1 tax to finance the largess of government. Thus, the following definitional terms are important to every self-employed individual.

## Business "Gross Income"

The term "gross income" for the No. 2 tax is quite different from that for the No. 1 tax. The No. 1 tax treats an individual's income from all sources worldwide as tax reportable on page 1 of Form 1040 (U.S. Individual Income Tax Return). To avoid confusion between the income term for the two taxes, the No. 1 tax uses the phrase: "total" gross income. Here, "total" means all incomes . . . from all sources . . . wheresoever/howsoever derived.

Altogether, total gross income encompasses 15 different classes of income [IRC Sec. 61(a)]. Of this number, only one is classed as "gross income derived from business" [Sec. 61(a)(2)]. Thus, business gross income is a much narrower term than is generally associated with the word "income" for No. 1 tax purposes.

Business gross income applies strictly to the participative (nonpassive) personal-service income generated by the owner or owners of a trade or business. Tax technically, it is **nonemployee compensation** for one's personal services. It is this personal-service income to which the No. 2 tax (for social security and medicare) applies.

In descriptive outline form, business gross income consists of the following sequential steps:

1. Gross receipts or sales
2. LESS returns and allowances
3. LESS cost of goods sold
4. PLUS other related income
5. Equals: GROSS INCOME

Here, the phrase "other related income" includes various kinds of miscellaneous business income, such as scrap sales, recovered bad debts, credits and adjustments, incidental commissions and overrides, referral fees, and the like.

For instructional focus purposes, we present in Figure 2.1 the essence of business gross income as distinguished from the total gross income of an individual. There is no point in arbitrarily or carelessly enhancing your business gross income. If you do, you are increasing your double taxation stake. Very few people enjoy double taxation on the same income.

## Less the "Deductions Allowed"

In the foregoing definition of net earnings from self-employment, the phrase: *gross income . . . less the deductions allowed* appears. What are the "deductions allowed"? The clear

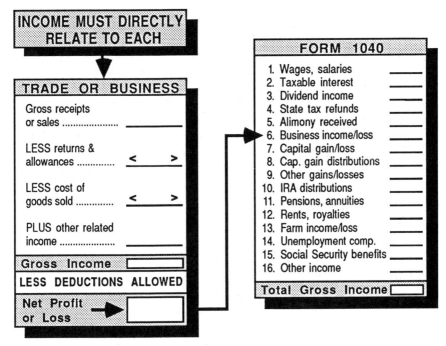

**Fig. 2.1 - Distinction of 'Business' from 'Total' Gross Income**

implication is that not all business expenses are allowed. So, what expenses are allowed as business deductions?

The most authoritative answer to this question is Section 162 of the tax code, and the regulations thereunder.

Section 162 is titled: *Trade or Business Expenses*. Its very first sentence: In General, reads—

*(a) There shall be allowed as a deduction all the ordinary and necessary expenses paid or incurred during the taxable year in carrying on any trade or business, including . . . [but not including . . .]*

The key phrase here is "**all** the ordinary and necessary expenses" for **carrying on** your business. This is amplified in Regulation 1.162-1(a): Business Expenses, which reads in pertinent part—

*Business expenses deductible from gross income include the ordinary and necessary expenditures **directly connected with** or pertaining to the taxpayer's trade or business. . . . Among the items included are management expenses, commissions, labor, supplies, incidental repairs, operating expenses of automobiles used in the trade or business, traveling expenses while away from home **solely in the pursuit** of a trade or business, advertising and other selling expenses, [certain] insurance premiums, and rentals for the use of business property. . . . The full amount of allowable deduction . . . is deductible, even though such expenses exceed the gross income derived during the taxable year from such business. [Emphasis added.]*

There are regulatory cross-references to other sections of the IR Code where, for specific types of business, other deductions are allowed (in whole or part). For items **not** deductible, there is a "no-no list" of 27 separate categories in Sections 261 through 280H. Section 162 itself contains several subsections of nondeductibles.

We'll cover deductible business expenses in more detail in Chapter 9: Net Profit or Loss. In the meantime, we just want you to recognize that not all self-alleged "business expenses" are automatically and fully deductible.

## Meaning of "Trade or Business"

As generally understood, a "trade or business" is some entrepreneurial activity carried on regularly for livelihood or profit. The "carrying on" aspect implies a more or less full-time attention to the business with the good faith intention of making a profit, as opposed to an activity engaged in purely for self-satisfaction. There must be some real evidence of economic motivation.

While an activity may seem to an individual to be a business, the IRS may determine that:

(1) the activity is a hobby, in which case the not-for-profit restrictions apply;

(2) the individual is an investor, in which case various passive loss and capital loss rules apply;

(3) the individual is an employee whose unreimbursed business expenses are allowed as personal itemized deduction to the extent

that they exceed 2 percent of the individual's adjusted gross income; or

(4) the activity is a sham, having no economic substance other than its tax benefits, in which case no related expenses are allowed.

More technically, Section 1402(c) defines the term "trade or business" as—

*When used with reference to self-employment income or net earnings from self-employment, [it] shall have the same meaning as when used in section 162 (relating to trade or business expenses), except that such term shall not include—*

*(1) the performance of the functions of a public office;*

*(2) the performance of service by an individual as an employee;*

*(3) the performance of service by an individual as an "employee representative" . . . in connection with or incidental to railroad transportation and railway labor organizations;*

*(4) the performance of service by a duly ordained, commissioned, or licensed minister of a church in the exercise of his ministry;*

*(5) the performance of service by an individual in the exercise of his profession or a Christian Science practitioner; or*

*(6) the performance of service by an individual during the period for which an exemption [from the No. 2 tax] is effective with respect to . . . a member of a recognized religious sect or division thereof.*

The idea behind Section 1402(c) is that, in order to be treated as being in a trade or business, one has to get out and hustle for business entirely on his own. If he is protected or sheltered in any way — such as being an IRS official or employee — he is not in a trade or business. Thus, being in a recognized profession or occupation is not the same as being self-employed in a trade or business.

**Husband and Wife Business**

In the latter part of Chapter 1: General Requirements, we extolled the benefits of husband and wife working together in a self-employed business. (Recall Figure 1.4.) This is fine from a business operations point of view. But when viewed in terms of the No. 2 tax on the net earnings, who pays it: the husband or the wife?

The No. 2 tax is ascribed to one individual only. It is not ascribed to both spouses jointly, even though the spouses may file a joint Form 1040. The self-employment tax Schedule SE that accompanies Form 1040 says—

*Name of person with self-employment income.*

It does not say: "Names of persons" (plural). Thus, in a husband and wife business, there has to be some agreement as to which of the two is the entrepreneurial (self-employed) spouse.

In separate property states, the allocation of spousal self-employment income is self-resolving. But in community property states, the income is state-law presumed as being attributable to both spouses. However, this state-law presumption is overridden by subsection 1402(a)(5)(A) of the federal tax code.

Subsection 1402(a)(5)(A) specifically says—

*If any of the income derived from a trade or business . . . is community income under community property laws applicable to such income, all of the gross income and deductions attributable to such trade or business shall be treated as [that] of the husband unless the wife exercises substantially all of the management and control of such trade or business, in which case all of such gross income and deductions shall be treated as [that] of the wife.*

This makes it pretty clear. The self-employment income is attributable to only one spouse: he or she who exercises the substantial portion of management and control (over the business).

In some cases, it is advantageous for each spouse to carve out a piece of the business for himself/herself. This is especially desirable if each spouse wants to build up separately his/her own *contribution base* in the Social Security System. To accomplish this, there need to be two side-by-side (husband and wife) self-employed businesses. We depict such an arrangement in Figure 2.2.

The overall effect of the Figure 2.2 arrangement is that, for No. 1 tax purposes, there is just one business. But for No. 2 tax purposes, there is a separate business for the husband, and a separate business for the wife. This adds some complication to the overall business accounting, but not inordinately so.

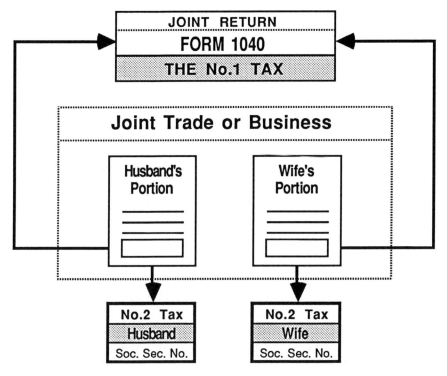

**Fig. 2.2 - Separate No.2 Taxes for Self-Employed Spouses**

### Partnership Business

In its general participative form, a partnership is treated as two or more self-employed individuals engaging in a common trade or business. Although there is no statutory limit to the number of self-employeds who can get together to form a general partnership, the practical limit is five.

In a partnership of five self-employed individuals, each is a part owner of the business. Yet, each is responsible and co-liable for the activities of the others. This is so because each partner is entitled to his/her *distributive share* of the income and deductions of the business. Consequently, with five owners of a business, there would be "five bosses." Unless the partners are fully business-compatible with each other, things could get out of hand. This is why five is the practical limit to the number of self-employed individuals in a general partnership.

On the subject of partnerships, Section 1402(a) makes two points. The first point is that—

*The term "net earnings from self-employment" means the gross income derived by an individual from any trade or business carried on by such individual, less the deductions allowed . . . which are attributable to . . . his distributive share (whether or not distributed) of income or loss . . . from any trade or business carried on by a partnership of which he is a member.*

This portion of the tax code addresses the "distributive share" of a partnership business and treats it as net earnings from self-employment, by each member of the partnership.

The second partnership point made is in subsection 1402(a)(5)(B), namely—

*If any portion of a partner's distributive share of the ordinary income or loss from a trade or business carried on by a partnership is community income or loss under the community property laws applicable to such share, all such distributive share shall be included in computing the net earnings from self-employment of such partner, and no part of such share shall be taken into account in computing the net earnings from self-employment of the spouse of such partner.*

In other words, each member of a partnership, whether married or unmarried, whether in a community property or separate property state, shall regard his/her distributive share (of the partnership income or loss) as his/her separate self-employment net earnings. This net earnings, of course, is subject to a separate No. 2 tax on the partnership member.

## Statutory Exemptions Limited

Not every self-employed individual is enthralled with the No., 2 tax. Some such individuals feel that they are self-disciplined enough that they can provide for their own old age, retirement, and disability. They resent the government — the IRS and the courts, particularly — mandating a tax on them for alleged old-age purposes.

Over the years since 1954 (when the No. 2 tax was first mandated against self-employeds), many hundreds of self-employeds have sought to sponsor intelligent alternatives to the No. 2 tax. But the Congress, the President, the IRS, and the courts, all adamantly refuse to consider any self-directed alternative whatsoever. It is not a matter of the merits of an alternative; it is simply an issue of power: taxing power. As a result, exceptions to the No. 2 tax are severely limited.

There are only two statutory exceptions to the dreaded social tax. One exception is Section 1402(e); this applies only to practicing clergy and non-vow-of-poverty religious orders. The second exception is Section 1402(g); this applies only to members of two particular sects: Amish and Mennonites. Each exception requires the self-employed individual to file with the IRS a formal "Application for Exemption From Self-Employment Tax."

Practicing clergy (ministers, rabbis, members of religious orders, and Christian Science practitioners) may file IRS Form 4361. This form requires that the applicant certify that he/she is—

*conscientiously opposed (because of religious principles) to the acceptance of any public insurance that makes payments in the event of death, disability, old age, or retirement; or that makes payments toward the cost of, or provides services for, medical care.*

If approved by the IRS, the exemption applies **only to** the applicant's ministerial earnings. Other forms of self-employment by the same individual are not umbrellaed with Form 4361.

For members of Amish, Mennonite, and similar sects — if the sect has been in existence continuously since 1950 — exemption Form 4029 may be used. This form requires a "conscientious objection" statement similar to Form 4361. It also requires that the religious group to which the applicant belongs provide a reasonable level of living for its dependent members. The applicant must also certify that he/she has never received any social security or medicare benefits, and that he/she waives all rights to any such benefits in the future.

## Section 1403:  Insurance Contributions?

Cynicism towards the No. 2 tax is furthered by Section 1403 of the Internal Revenue Code. This is perhaps the shortest section of that code. It consists of just two sentences, namely: 1403(a) and 1403(b).

Sentence (a) says—

*This chapter* [Chapter 2: Tax on Self-Employment Income] *may be cited as the "Self-Employment **Contributions** Act of 1954."* [Emphasis added.]

If the No. 2 tax is a "contributions act," why is it made mandatory as a tax? The word *contribution* generally signifies the giving of something voluntarily for a charitable cause. There is nothing voluntary and nothing charitable when the government imposes its protection as a tax.

Sentence (b) says—

*For provisions relating to returns, see section 6017.*

Well, let's take a look at Section 6017. What does it say? That section is titled: ***Self-Employed Tax Returns***. It reads in full as—

*Every individual (other than a nonresident alien individual) having net earnings from self-employment of $400 or more for the taxable year shall make a return with respect to the self-employment tax imposed by chapter 2. In the case of a husband and wife filing a joint return under section 6013* [Joint Returns of Income Tax], *the tax imposed by chapter 2 shall not be computed on the aggregate income but shall be the **sum of the taxes** computed under such chapter on the separate self-employment income of each spouse*. [Emphasis added.]

So, now we have **two** No. 2 tax impositions: one on the husband's self-employment earnings and another on the wife (if she is separately self-employed). These two No. 2 taxes are **in addition to** the No. 1 tax on the joint incomes of husband and wife.

On a joint return, ordinarily, the No. 1 tax does not apply until the combined incomes exceed $10,000. But, in the case of the No. 2 tax, the imposition applies to $400 or more of the net earnings of each spouse.

# 3

# KEEPING PROPER RECORDS

> Every Person Liable For ANY TAX Imposed By The IRS . . . "Shall Keep Such Records, Render Such Statements, And Make Such Returns" . . . As Is Appropriate To His/Her Trade Or Business [IRC Sec. 6001]. Your Bank Records, Deposit Slips, And Cancelled Checks Comprise The Foundation For This Effort. Your "Capital Account" Consists Of Various Expenditures Which Are Not Deductible Immediately, And In Some Cases Not Deductible Until The Business Is Terminated. Your Ultimate Recordkeeping Goal Is Codification By Specific Categories Which Integrate Directly Into Your Various Tax Forms And Schedules: Income And Other.

It takes a lot of gumption and hard work to get a self-employment business going. There are many fits and starts. Mistakes are made. Significant amounts of "front money" are required. A product or service has to be developed and advertised. Customers and clients have to be solicited and nourished. Some customers will pay promptly; some will pay late; and some will not pay at all. During all of this time, there is money going out and money coming in. And, throughout it all, there is your livelihood to be maintained.

As if it weren't enough of a struggle getting a business going on its own, there are those "silent partners" — the IRS (and state and local taxing agencies) — wanting the first bite out of every dollar crumb that comes your way.

Tax agencies are great hindsighters. They come on the scene, usually, two or three years after your struggles. They pounce on you for perfect records in an imperfect world. They can "cite the book" on what you were supposed to have done about keeping records. But they can't envision the trials and tribulations that you have endured. Their greed for tax revenue totally blinds them to the realities of small business life. Nevertheless, you do have a *duty* to keep responsible records of your business affairs.

Thus, in this chapter, we want to create in you the *frame of mind* for establishing and maintaining good accounting records. Your frame of mind in knowing what is important and what is not so important is far more valuable to business success than penny-by-penny bookkeeping, bean counting, and "keeping everything" for record purposes. To get into the right frame of mind, it is helpful to adopt the philosophy that—

*Nothing is perfect in an imperfect world: the IRS notwithstanding.*

## Why Records Important

Why do we say that you have a "duty" to keep responsible records?

There are three reasons, namely:

**One.** To judge for yourself that the business is providing the kind of livelihood that you seek.

**Two.** To defend yourself against lawsuits, regulatory inspections, insurer investigations, and complaints by customers and suppliers.

**Three.** To determine your *correct* net earnings for the No. 2 tax. The IRS wants to make this tax as high as possible. Doing so, it can automatically extract a much higher No. 1 tax from you.

There are certain records that you want to keep temporarily for yourself. You need to do so to determine how your business is doing. For example, of gross sales or receipts, you may want a product or customer breakdown to determine what segment of your business is most profitable. You don't want to spend advertising money on a market niche which doesn't produce any significant income for you. Similarly, you need to keep for yourself certain accounts receivable (what customers owe you) and accounts payable (what you owe to suppliers and others). You need these kinds of records for cash flow analysis, and for making sensible business decisions. None of these kinds of records are of much interest to tax collectors.

There are also those records that you need for defensive legal purposes, insurance investigations, and regulatory inspections. You never know when some customer, supplier, contractor, or co-worker may file a lawsuit against you. For your own protection, you need certain records of your promises and pledges, of your contracts and warranties, and of your business conduct and procedures. Similarly, you need other records for insurance agents and adjusters, and for periodic visits by regulatory inspectors such as fire, health, safety, local licensing, and so on. Except for the cost of preparing these records, tax collectors are not too interested in them.

But when it comes to keeping *tax records*, you face a different ballgame. The tax code is pretty emphatic. It says in no uncertain terms that you are expected to keep adequate records on all of your business income, and of all your expenditures which you claim as deductions against your income. The bottom-line purpose of this recordkeeping is to establish — and substantiate — your net earnings from self-employment. Poor records in this regard automatically mean higher taxes than necessary.

Since this is a tax book, we are only going to discuss the kinds of tax records that you need for preparing and supporting the entries on your annual income tax return. Many of these records will also serve for sales tax purposes, property tax purposes, excise tax purposes, and withholding tax purposes.

### Your "Official Notice"

You may not realize it, but you have already been given official notice to keep proper records. The notice was not sent to you personally, of course. It is a public notice that was published in the Federal Register as far back as 1954. It is now firmly embodied in the Internal Revenue Code as Section 6001. This section is titled: *Notice or Regulations Requiring Records, Statements, and Special Returns*.

As pertinent to our discussion, Section 6001 reads—

*Every person liable for **any tax** imposed by* [the IR Code], *or for the* [withholding] *collection thereof, **shall** keep such records, render such statements, make such returns, and comply with such rules or regulations as the* [IRS] *may from time to time prescribe. Whenever in the judgment of the* [IRS] *it is necessary,* [it] *may require any person, **by notice served upon such person** or by regulations, to make such returns, render such statements, or keep such records, as the* [IRS] ***deems sufficient** to show whether or not such person is liable for tax under* [the IR Code]. [Emphasis added.]

This is quite an order, and is dictatorial in sound. The "tax god" speaketh. It applies to every self-employed individual generating $400 or more in net earnings, in any given year. Unfortunately, one doesn't always know until the end of the year what his net earnings will be. Thus, the practical effect of the official notice is that proper records must be kept for $100 or more of any business income.

As to the *form of records* required, Regulation 31.6001-1(a) says—

*The records required . . . shall be kept accurately, but no particular form is required for keeping the records. Such forms and systems of accounting shall be used as will enable the* [IRS] *to ascertain whether liability for tax is incurred and, if so, the amount thereof.*

As to *retention of records*, Regulation 1.6001-1(e) says—

*The books or records required . . . shall be kept at all times available for inspection by authorized internal revenue officers or employees, and shall be retained so long as the contents thereof may become material in the administration of any internal revenue law.*

In other words, every business "shall keep" such records, statements, returns, etc., as is pertinent to that business. No official format of recordkeeping is prescribed. Such records should be retained as long as they may be needed for countering various assessments by the IRS. This leaves these matters to the independent judgment of each functioning business owner.

## Typical Mistakes Made

To get you in the right frame of mind for preparing the kind of records that are appropriate to your business, we first want to review some of the typical recordkeeping mistakes made by self-employeds. Costly mistakes are made because most taxpayers cannot envision what the IRS is expressly looking for. It focuses primarily on tax accountable INCOME, and only secondarily on deductions. By maximizing your taxable income, and minimizing your allowable deductions, great amounts of revenue will gush into federal coffers.

The first typical mistake is confusion over what constitutes tax accountable income. Many businesses have to borrow money, use lines of credit, tap into personal savings, seek interest-free loans from family and friends, or solicit pre-inheritance gifts from parents and other benefactors. Funds from all of these sources go into the business account for operating purposes. This is NOT tax accountable income generated by the business itself. Consequently, each business owner has to establish his own system for tracking borrowed and nontaxable money used in the business. In this regard, we offer some specific suggestions below.

Another typical recordkeeping mistake is ordinary procrastination and forgetfulness. Harried business owners don't have the time to sit down and painstakingly record every penny in and every penny out. There are more important — and more interesting — things to do. So they put off . . . and put off. Correcting these bad habits requires a "holding system" (of envelopes, folders, or boxes) for collecting records daily. This is followed periodically (weekly, bi-weekly, monthly) by a scheduled sit-down time (after regular business hours) for reviewing and posting the records into tax-characterized categories. For this, strict self-discipline is required. Whatever your excuses may be, proper records MUST BE KEPT.

A very common mistake is "keeping everything." This is done in the hope that one can find the right record or statement when it is demanded of him, months and years later. A "keeping everything" system simply won't work for tax purposes. No IRS examiner is going to probe through your boxes and boxes of records to find what he or she wants. It is your job to segregate your records into specific tax categories. Then, for each category, run an adding machine tape and attach it to each category. The dollar magnitude of a category often determines the extent of IRS interest.

Another mistake is assuming that the IRS is going to understand your business problems and be empathetic towards you. The IRS doesn't give a hoot about your business affairs, or whether you make good sales or bad sales, or that you have suffered setbacks due to a slow economy, lawsuits, warranty claims, or regulatory orders. It just doesn't care! All the IRS really cares about is identifying the maximum income that it can tax.

Still another mistake is keeping a "double set of books" pertaining to income. As we indicated earlier, there are many records that you need for purposes other than for tax accounting. When these records focus on the income side of your accounting ledgers, watch out! The IRS will start suspecting that you are hauling in tons of money and keeping it off the tax books. This is particularly true when you have bartering arrangements, cash transactions (paper money and coin), wagering-type activities, trade-ins, exchanges, and so on. When it comes to suspicions of income off-the-tax-books, IRS agents are superbly trained as blood hounds.

And, finally, perhaps the most common mistake of all conscientious taxpayers is the confusing — and mixing up — of personal and business expenditures. What may be a justified business expense in your mind is often treated as a disallowed personal expense in the IRS's mind. This is particularly true of travel, entertainment, insurance, family-use items, vehicles, and equipment used both for personal and business purposes. The need for separating personal expenditures from business expenditures winds its way through all tax laws affecting self-employeds. Unless an expenditure is motivated **primarily by business necessity**, it will be automatically disallowed by the IRS as a personal expense. Here, good self-discipline is required when recording these matters.

## Business Bank Account

If you want to start off right, we suggest that you set up a unitary business bank account. Preferably do so with a separate financial institution apart from all other accounts (checking, savings, investment) that you might have. Set it up in a way that it becomes your sole depository of all of your trade or business income. Even if you have several trade or businesses, set up **only one** account. There is a special reason for this.

Multiple bank accounts for multiple businesses give the IRS the impression that you are "laundering money." Particularly if you are moving it around in such a way that disguises its true source and true amount. This is what the drug lords and crime syndicates do. If you do have several legitimate businesses, you can keep separate nonbank income records for each business, then allocate the total bank deposits in your one account, proportionately at the end of each year. Whatever you do, you want to create the impression that you are trying to do things right. One bank for depositing all business income will do it.

Make it a checking-only bank account. The small amount of interest that you might otherwise earn is not worth the computer-matching headaches to which the IRS will subject you. All bank account interest is separately reported to the IRS (on Form 1099-INT) irrespective of whether it comes from a business account, personal account, or investment account. If you still want that interest, transfer the excess balances in your business checking account over to your personal savings. After all, it is *your* money, although, at times, the IRS treats all business income as its own.

Whatever you do, make sure that the origin of each deposit in your business account is clearly identified. For example, if you are using borrowed money, gifted money, or prior savings money in your business, be sure to identify on your copy of each deposit slip the origin of that money. The same applies to nontaxable money such as return of capital, tax-exempt interest, and nontaxable refunds. If you do not carefully earmark each of your nonbusiness income deposits, as we depict in Figure 3.1, the IRS will treat all deposits in your business account as being derived solely from your business.

### Keep Bank Records Available

As a self-employed business owner, your business bank deposits are viewed virtually as "public records." It is not that they are open to the general public, but that they are open to the IRS at its whim. Don't refuse the IRS's access to your bank records on the premises of privacy, constitutional grounds, etc. The U.S. Constitution is **not** required reading by IRS agents.

The IRS's rationale is that all banks are government-regulated entities. As such, they are required by federal law to keep record of all deposits into your account, and of all withdrawals from it. Therefore, the bank-prepared records are *third-party* records. That is, they can be inspected by the IRS with or without notice to you . . . and with or without your approval.

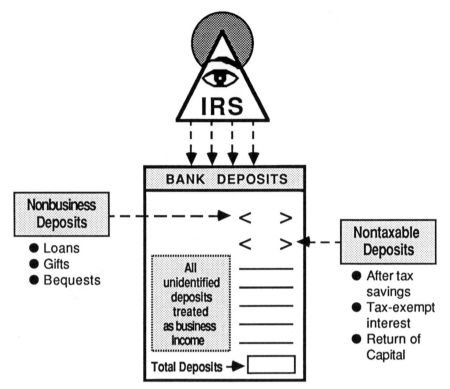

**Fig. 3.1 - Importance of Identifying Each Bank Deposit**

Ordinarily, the IRS will not go to your bank and seize your records without first requesting them from you. This means that you should keep your business bank records readily available at all times. By "bank records" we mean deposit slips, monthly bank statements, and the cancelled checks written on the business account. Despite our modern era of all-electronic banking, when tax push comes to tax shove, those old-fashioned bank records will stand you well.

If the business bank that you choose does not provide you with hard-copy deposit slips, monthly statements, and cancelled checks, find a bank that will. Pay whatever extra charge is necessary (it *is* deductible). Keep these records available for IRS scrutiny at any time. They become your *foundation category* of proper records for tax purposes. We reiterate this in Figure 3.2.

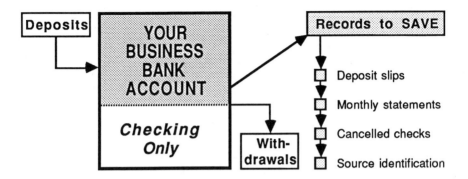

**NOTE:** *"Paperless" (computer) deposits and withdrawals cause painful tracking problems for tax accounting.*

**Fig. 3.2 - Your "Foundation Category" of Important Tax Records**

## Understanding Capitalization

There are many legitimate business expenditures which cannot be deducted in the year paid or incurred. Even if the expenditure is paid immediately from the business gross income, it cannot be deducted immediately. In fact, it may not be deductible at all. Or, at best, it can only be deducted over a period of years — sometimes over many years. This is the "capitalization" principle that the IRS uses to characterize certain expenditures so as to defer their deductibility. Understanding this principle is important for identifying those cost-of-business items that the IRS will "pick at" for maximizing your No. 1 and No. 2 taxes.

In general, a capital item is an asset of the business which is *not consumed* in or by the business within the year in which it is acquired. For example, you buy a piece of equipment that you must have for running your business. Being a small operator with no long-established credit rating, you have to pay cash for the equipment. Suppose the item cost $35,000. Do you get an immediate deduction for it against your business gross income?

No. You do not.

You have to allocate the $35,000 cost to each year that the equipment can be productively used. Suppose the equipment has a useful life of 10 years. This means, then, that the allowable deduction each year (assuming straight-line cost recovery) would be

$3,500 ($35,000 ÷ 10 years).  The remaining $31,500 ($35,000 - $3,500) may be recovered over the next nine consecutive years.

Guess what happens?  A cash flow problem arises.  You paid $35,000 for a business item for which you get only a $3,500 deduction.  This makes you "cash short" by $31,500.  Yet, you still have to pay income tax (No. 1 **and** No. 2) on $31,500 that you no longer have.

Now, you know why the IRS fights every business owner tooth and nail over capitalization.  It wants to recharacterize every expenditure possible as a **capital item** rather than accept it as a current expense.  A "current expense" is an expenditure which is fully consumed, or essentially so, in the year incurred and, therefore, is fully deductible.  Whether an expenditure is a capital item or an expense item often is purely an intellectual call.  In its hyperactive capitalization dance, the IRS can be quite mean spirited.

Over the years, Congress has sought to soften the IRS sting by enacting, and amending, the following sections of the tax code:

Sec. 167 — Depreciation
Sec. 168 — Accelerated cost recovery
Sec. 178 — Amortization of a lease
Sec. 195 — Start-up expenditures
Sec. 248 — Organizational expenditures
Sec. 263 — Capital expenditures
Sec. 263A — Capitalization and inclusion in inventory

But these and other sections of the tax code cannot address every conceivable expenditure situation that arises.  As a result, each business owner is left to fend for himself/herself on capital accounting matters.

## Capital Account Records

This brings us now to the second major category of recordkeeping, namely:  capital account records.  Your "capital account" is your cumulative investment in the business in the form of fixed assets.  With adjustments over time, it represents the *book value* of your business should you decide someday to sell, exchange, or terminate the business.

A complete set of capital account records would consist of the following categories of items:

1. Nondepreciable assets
   — land, goodwill, licenses
2. Depreciable assets
   — structures, equipment, vehicles
3. Amortizable costs
   — covenants, customer lists, leaseholds
4. Inventory of goods
   — merchandise, materials, work-in-process
5. Other intangibles
   — accounts receivable, prepaid deposits
6. Depletable assets
   — natural resources, timber, oil & gas

By and large, categories 1, 2, and 3 represent the most common form of capitalization attention by small businesses. Categories 5 and 6 are more transitory in nature, and are nowhere near the dollar magnitude of 1, 2, and 3 for self-employeds. Category 4 is applicable only where merchandise is purchased for resale, or where products are manufactured and sold.

We depict in Figure 3.3 the capital account groupings that you should prepare records on, as appropriate to your own business. For each item that you enter into each capital subaccount, your primary documentation therewith is your acquisition invoice. This constitutes your initial cost. To this cost, you add other related costs, such as title fees, freight in, installation, preproduction testing, and so on. We highly recommend that all of these costs be a direct appendage to the capital account records for the year of *placement in service* of the asset. Many business owners tend to collect these invoices and costs in their "accounts payable" files rather than directly attaching them to their capital accounts records. Ready access to cost-of-assets data is one of the key features that we try to portray in Figure 3.3.

Just a word about nondepreciable assets. Nondepreciable assets are those which you acquire and use in the business, but you get no writeoff — no deduction whatever — for them. This is because, supposedly, such assets have *no determinable life*. A good example of this indetermination is land. You buy a parcel of land to erect a building on it for conducting your business. The land itself will always be there (except for erosions, earthquakes, and excavations). For tax purposes, it doesn't depreciate. It just sits there on your books . . . forever.

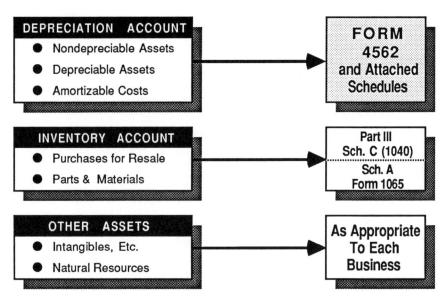

**Fig. 3.3 - Capital Account Groupings of Assets Used in Business**

## Slow Moving Inventory

Another asset that just sort of sits on your books is inventory. The term "inventory" applies to those goods, products, and other items that you buy, fabricate, or service with the intention of selling them at a profit. If the items are slow moving or don't sell at all, you have money tied up in your business for which there is no tax writeoff.

We all know that the intention of making a profit and actually making a profit are two different things. Some inventory just doesn't sell. What do you do? And what records do you need to document what you do?

One option you have is that you can always leave your unsold inventory sitting there on your books. Whatever you paid for it — as evidenced by purchase invoices and billing charges — becomes "tied up money." If for no other reason than for your own knowledge, you must have cumulative records on what that unsold inventory has cost you. You can't make sound business decisions without knowing what your costs are.

The only way to untie your money is to get rid of your unsold inventory somehow. Doing so, you reduce the gross income to the business.  This, in turn, means that you pay less tax (both No. 1 and No. 2).  By paying less income tax you, indirectly, recover the cost of your inventory unsold.

Getting rid of slow-moving or nonmoving inventory in a small business presents a problem.  If you put on a "fire sale," for example, you may depress the price of your good inventory.  The same applies to giving it away . . . even to charity.  A self-employed owner (whether sole proprietor or member of a partnership) gets no business deduction for charitable donations.  He may get a personal deduction but NOT a business deduction.

The only way to get a business deduction for slowmoving or nonmoving inventory is to *have it destroyed*!  Yes, we know:  this sounds harsh.  But it is a good tax solution to the dilemma of tied-up money.  By destroying the inventory, you cut down your income taxes proportionately.  When you do so, you had better have good records (why, when, by whom).

Destroying inventory should be done by a third party.  It should NOT be done by yourself.  You are a party-at-interest and, therefore, tax suspect.  Engage and pay some person or entity outside of your business to do the destruction for you.  Take photographs of your inventory before turning it over to the destruction vendor.  Have him give you a receipt for it.  Also have him sign an agreement that he will not try to reclaim, recycle, refurbish, and resell it.  When it is destroyed, have him send confirmation and evidence of the destruction.  You want rock solid substantiation of the destruction when the IRS, or some state or local agency, quizzes you.

In Figure 3.4, we summarize the records required when destroying inventory.  If you are in a business where selling inventory is the mainstay of gross income, good inventory accounting and recordkeeping is a major responsibility in and of itself.

## Compensation to Others

Ideally, a self-employed business should have no employees.  The moment you have one employee, you have all the record-keeping, all the withholdings, all the social security, all the medicare, all the insurance, . . . and all the bureaucracy of any major company with thousands of employees.  Government is the absolute "protector" of every employee in the U.S.  You dare have one

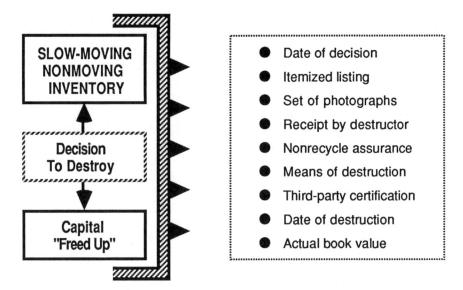

**Fig. 3.4 - Documentation to Prove Destruction of Inventory**

employee and the wrath of many government agencies — not just the IRS — will be down upon you.

Still, you cannot run a business without paying compensation to persons other than yourself for services rendered. How do you do this without having employees? There are at least five ways, but none spare you all recordkeeping on the compensation paid.

The five ways for avoiding employees are contacts with—

1. *Established businesses.* Subcontract with them to do defined portions of your business effort on a phase-by-phase basis.
2. *Employment agencies and "job shops."* Contract for worker specialists on a part-time, job-by-job basis, where the agency remains the employer and takes care of all payroll paperwork.
3. *Outside vendors and free-lancers.* These are persons who have niche specialties and work for many persons and entities on a catch-as-catch-can basis; such persons are self-employed in their own right.
4. *Independent contractors.* Regularly self-employed persons and others who may be "moonlighting" from regular

employment. They also may be unemployed or under-employed persons seeking, perhaps, to go into business for themselves.

5. *Commission payees.* These are sales representatives, direct sellers, prospectors, distributors, and others whose compensation is a specified percentage of the "list price" of the goods, products, and services sold by them, or for which they have been instrumental in causing the sale.

In all five cases above, if the person or entity whom you engage is **other than** a full-fledged corporation, you have to prepare — for each payee — a Form 1099-MISC. The "MISC" is "miscellaneous income." This is a tax information form for reporting to the IRS (and to state and local tax agencies) all payments for compensation amounting to $600 or more, each taxable year. Although this form consists of some 12 entry dollar boxes, the most common entry box used by self-employed businesses is Box 7: *Nonemployee compensation $_____.*

Form 1099-MISC can markedly cut down on your record-keeping for compensation paid to others. But you still have to keep certain minimum records. For example, you must insist on obtaining each payee's correct name, correct address, and correct tax identification number (TIN). If any one of these items is incorrect, you will be required to withhold 20% of the gross compensation and turn it over to the IRS. The process of this withholding opens up a whole can of worms of federal tax deposits, transmittal forms, and payroll accounting . . . just like a regular employer.

## Simplified Expense Records

Every self-employed knows something about keeping records on the expenses necessary for operating his business: advertising, travel, utilities, repairs, supplies, fees, and so on. These are costs which are consumed/absorbed in the business, and which have no book value or assets beyond one year. As such, they are fully deductible against the business gross income.

Unfortunately, some self-employed individuals become quite obsessed about expense records. They record every little penny ante amount that is disbursed. This is self-enslavement. It detracts from the excitement of making money, and doing constructive things in life. Even if you kept perfect records and matched every penny, you would not satisfy the IRS. It will pick, pick away at you, suspecting that you are trying to hide or get away with something, by being so perfect.

To keep life simple while forging ahead in your business, we offer the following suggestions (beyond those previously cited):

**One**. For expenses less than $10 per transaction, pay by cash. don't clutter up your files with a lot of petty receipts. Guess at the cumulative amounts at the end of the year, and add them as "petty cash" expenditures in the tax-appropriate categories.

**Two**. For disbursements of $10 or more, pay by business check. In the lower, left-hand corner of the check, enter a short description of the transaction. Your cancelled check becomes your receipt. Make the payee's name (the "Pay to the order of") legible and self-explanatory.

**Three**. For business travel and entertainment, use a *business* credit card. Have a totally separate credit card for this purpose. When given a receipt for your transaction, take time out to write on the back thereof the business purpose of your expenditure. Pay your monthly credit card bill with a business check.

**Four**. Where you are invoiced for expense items of $100 or more, SAVE THE INVOICES. If a billing is less than $100, and you have a cancelled check for the same item, you can throw the "small invoices" away. Again, don't clutter up your records with trivia.

**Five**. If posting your expenses on a weekly spreadsheet ledger is too much for you (either by hand or by computer), set yourself up an envelope or folder system. Label the envelopes or folders by expense categories appropriate to your business. Then, as they pass through your hands, toss those cancelled checks and invoices into those envelopes or folders. Once every three months or so, review your recordkeeping system . . . and revise it as necessary.

Incidentally, keeping track of your tax records on your home computer is NOT ACCEPTABLE by the IRS as substantiation of your recordkeeping. The burden of proof is on you to come up with hard-copy stuff, such as good old-fashioned cancelled checks, purchase invoices, billing statements, and paid receipts.

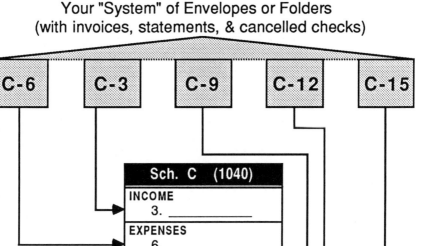

Your "System" of Envelopes or Folders
(with invoices, statements, & cancelled checks)

Your Business Tax Schedule

**Fig. 3.5 - Codifying Expenditures to Specific Lines on Return**

### Your Ultimate Goal

The general idea that we are trying to get across is that "keeping proper records" should be an integral part of your business. Your transactional activities should include a system of recordkeeping that you habitually and systematically do, without thinking about it. The system that you develop should not be one where you have to take special time out for reconstructing, segregating, and posting. Your system should be one that, ideally, "takes care of itself." Our suggestions above are presented with this automaticity in mind.

There are only two persons that you have to satisfy for recordkeeping purposes. One is yourself. You need to keep some track of your income and disbursement to judge how your business is doing.

Your business checkbook balance gives you a photoflash of your daily profit or loss.

The second person you have to satisfy is a *nonperson*. It is a bureaucracy called the IRS and its affiliated tax agencies, state and local. This nonperson comes on the scene two or three years after the fact to demand more money — called "tax revenue" — from you. This nonperson does not assist you in your business; yet, it demands a dominant share of the profit therefrom.

Consequently, your ultimate goal is to develop a system of recordkeeping that integrates directly into your various tax returns: income and other. When your records are done, your tax returns are also done.

The way to do this is to code your expenditure categories with the same line numbers as they appear on your tax forms and schedules. For example, Schedule C, line 11 is: *Commissions and fees*. At the end of the year, package your appropriate nonemployee compensation as "C-11." Do likewise for all applicable lines on your tax return. We illustrate this tax coding idea in Figure 3.5.

Once you get the knack of tax coding your disbursement categories as you go along throughout the year, recordkeeping becomes synonymous with preparing your tax return for that year. This way, your tax return — at least the business portion of it — will be done in January of each year.

There is no need whatsoever for dread and procrastination. Furthermore, there is no need for requesting extensions of time to file your returns. Habitually requesting extensions of time to file gives the impression that you don't keep good records. Poor business recordkeeping translates directly into much higher taxes than are necessary.

# 4

# BUSINESS USE OF HOME

Section 280A(c) Sets The Tax Conditions For Deductibility Of Certain Expenses For Business Use Of Your Home. The Area(s) You Designate As Business Must Be Used REGULARLY And EXCLUSIVELY As: (a) Principal Place Of Business, (b) Meeting Place With Customers, (c) Storage Of Inventory, OR (d) Separate Business Structure. The Measured Square Footage Of All Designated Areas Establishes The "Business Use Percentage" Of Your Total Dwelling Unit. Form 8829 Is Used To Compute Your Allowable Deductions. These Are Allowed Only To The Extent That They Produce No Additional Net Loss On Your Business Schedule C.

Many self-employeds find it necessary to use portions of their personal residence for business purposes. This "necessity" arises from (a) economics, (b) convenience, and (c) efficiency. But, as with any endeavor, working out of one's home has advantages and disadvantages. The primary disadvantage is the stringency of the tax rules involved.

A person who is newly self-employed, or who is self-employed in a certain specialty, finds it economical to conduct the focal aspects of the business out of his or her home. The economics stems from the sharing of certain personal, family, and business expenses for shelter and utilities. But this "sharing" invokes the general disallowance rule of Sections 262 and 280A which we have to address herein.

The convenience of working at home is unsurpassed. A self-employed business is NOT an 8-hour-day, 5-days-a-week business. It's more like 12-hour days, 6-1/2 days a week. If one has to commute several miles or more from his home to his office, store, or shop to conduct business at odd hours, there is much lost time. Furthermore, in certain types of businesses, customers and clients like knowing that they can reach you at home during off hours. Off-hour access is one of the star competitive advantages that self-employeds have over traditional-type enterprises. Sometimes, though, this ready access for off-hour business can interfere with personal and family living.

There is no question that, if you can conduct the major portion of your business out of your home, you can make it into a very efficient operation. You are not dependent on the whims and vacillations of bosses, co-workers, suppliers, vendors, and government agents. You can organize your work routine, streamline your operation, and simplify your recordkeeping. If you are truly self-disciplined, you can institute a "clean desk" policy whereby everything has its place and is **in** its place. No more workplace disorder and confusion, as is typically found in offices, stores, and shops in local business districts.

So, in this chapter, we want to focus strictly on the tax rules for getting a legitimate deduction for your business-at-home expenditures. Doing so, we will excerpt the key tax code sections on point, and will describe in some detail the features of Form 8829: *Expenses for Business Use of Your Home*. If you are going to be self-employed and work extensively out of your home, this chapter is a MUST.

## Section 280A(c): Introduction

The IRS has always chafed at allowing any deduction against gross income for expenses incurred while working out of one's home. For some reason, this is an area of endeavor that tax agents simply can't comprehend as being a necessity of self-employment. Consequently, the IRS — as early as 1954 — has induced Congress to enact Section 262 of the IR Code. This section, titled: *Personal, Living, and Family Expenses*, says, in its subsection (a) that—

*Except as otherwise provided . . ., no deduction shall be allowed for personal, living, and family expenses.*

This is clear and concise: "no deductions shall be allowed."

With Section 262(a) as its mandate, the IRS has been quite successful at maximizing revenue by arbitrarily disallowing all business-use-of-home expenses.

Finally, Congress came to its senses in 1986 and amended a portion of the law it had enacted in 1975 disallowing expenses in connection with . . . *the use of a dwelling unit* [Sec. 280A]. It amended Section 280A to include a subsection (c): *Exceptions for Certain Business or Rental Use.* Paragraph (1) of subsection (c) is particularly pertinent at this point. There are also paragraph (2): Certain Storage Use, paragraph (4): Providing Day Care Services, and paragraph (5): Limitation on Deductions. We'll get to paragraphs (2), (4) and (5) later. Paragraph (3): Rental Use of Home, is beyond our discussion.

Paragraph (1) of Section 280A(c) reads in full as follows:

*(1) Subsection (a)* [relating to "no deduction allowed"] *shall not apply to any item to the extent such item is allocable to a portion of the dwelling unit which is used exclusively on a regular basis—*

*(A) as the principal place of business for any trade or business of the taxpayer,*

*(B) as a place of business which is used by patients, clients, or customers in meeting or dealing with the taxpayer in the normal course of his trade or business, or*

*(C) in the case of a separate structure which is not attached to the dwelling unit, in connection with the taxpayer's trade or business.*

Thus, right off, there is one of three alternative conditions to be met, in order to circle around the "no deduction allowed" mandate. Any one alternative will satisfy the exception provision; any two alternatives will satisfy; or any combination of all three. We'll discuss the exception alternatives one at a time.

## Regular and Exclusive Use

There is a basic umbrella requirement to be met for all alternatives (A), (B), and (C). That is, the designated (as business) portion of the dwelling unit must be used . . . *exclusively on a regular basis.* The is the "exclusive use" test which the IRS makes much ado about.

As defined in Regulation 1.280A-2(g), the test for exclusivity is met—

> *. . . only if there is no use of that portion of the unit at any time during the taxable year other than for business purposes.* [Emphasis added.]

This means that there can be no personal, family, or recreational use — at any time — of that portion of your home which you designate for business. Indications of nonbusiness use would be the existence of television, pool table, sofa bed, comfortable lounge, children's toys, storage of wearing apparel, and other accoutrements of everyday living. Temporary entry by family members and others for cleaning, maintenance, and repairs does not defeat the exclusivity test.

Regulation 1.280A-2(g) goes on to say that—

> *The phrase "a portion of the dwelling unit" refers to a room or other **separately identifiable space**; it is not necessary that the portion be marked off by a permanent partition.* [Furthermore], *the portion . . . may be used for more than one business purpose.* [Emphasis added.]

Regulation 1.280A-1(c)(1) defines a "dwelling unit" as—

> *A house, apartment, condominium, mobile home, boat, or similar property, which provides basic living accommodations such as sleeping space, toilet, and cooking facilities. A single structure may contain more than one dwelling unit. All structures and other property appurtenant to a dwelling unit . . . are considered part of the unit.*

What all of this is saying is that, if you designate a separately identifiable portion of your home for business use, and you use it regularly as such, it *may* qualify as business property. If so, the allocable expenses therewith would be deductible.

### Principal Place of Business

Once the umbrella test of exclusive use is met, the first statutory alternative is the "principal place" test. This is alternative (A), otherwise designated as Section 280A(c)(1)(A). This rule requires that the designated business-use portion of your home be the principal place for conducting your business. If your home is the only place where you conduct business, there is no interpretation problem. But suppose you have two or more places for doing business, which one is the principal place?

For example, suppose you make handcrafted items in your attached garage, or you prepare food specialties in your kitchen at home. When completed, you take the items to a public marketplace, or rented display stand, where they are sold. Where is your principal place of business: at home or at the display stand?

The IRS will rule that the display stand is your principal place of business. This follows because the display stand is the "focal point" of your income and is the spot where goods and services are provided to your customers.

On the other hand, suppose you own three laundromats in a citywide area. You engage independent contractors at each location to help customers, sell laundry products, and keep the places clean. You visit each of the three locations once a day. You empty the coin boxes, keep the changers full, replenish supplies, and post notices and instructions to customers and caretakers. There is no office or private phone at any of the laundromat locations. You do all of your ordering of supplies and replacement equipment; all of your record-keeping; all arrangements for repairs; all temporary coin storage; and all preparation of notices and operating instructions at your home. You go to your bank several times a week to deposit your coin collections. All total, you spend about five hours a day at home, going to the bank, visiting suppliers, and about three hours a day at the laundromats. Where is your principal place of business?

The IRS will argue that the laundromat where you collected the most money during the year is your place of business. But various courts have used the "dominant portion" and "facts and circumstances" tests to differ with the IRS.

A sensible approach to the principal place decision is an intelligent weighing of various business factors. Among the factors that the IRS and the Tax Court will consider are the following:

1. The length of time spent at home on business compared with the time spent elsewhere.
2. The importance of the business functions performed at home, compared with those performed elsewhere.
3. The necessity and suitability of an office at home, compared with its incidental availability elsewhere.

4. The availability of adequate office, shop, or storage space, including telephone and business privacy, at locations other than at one's home.
5. The amount of expertise, and the nature of the organizational and management activities, essential to conducting the business, relative to those activities that generate the income.

Many of the IRS assertions of your principal place of business are based on its hasty judgment calls. It is so easy for the IRS to say "No." But as a dedicated self-employed, you have to be more forceful in standing up to the IRS. Towards this end, the "facts and circumstances" that you should be loaded with are presented in Figure 4.1. The principal place test is the most controversial of the three Section 280A(c) alternatives.

## Meeting Place With Customers

Alternative (B) [Sec. 280A(c)(1)(B)] provides that even though your home is not your principal place of business, it may still qualify for business deductions if you meet regularly there with customers, clients, or patients. Such a meeting place symbolizes the dominant activities of any business. Customers, clients, and patients are the ones who provide you with income. Whether they pay you at home, pay you from their homes, pay by credit card, or make direct deposits in your business bank account, if you *meet* with them in the regular course of business in your home, you qualify.

The meetings must be face to face. At the significant stages of your business transactions, you and your customers must be physically present with each other. It is not sufficient that your principal contacts are by phone or through third-party arrangements. This physical meeting at home can cause qualifying problems for such self-employeds as physicians (who meet their patients in a hospital), attorneys (who meet their clients in court), and real estate agents (who meet their customers at title company offices).

In particular occupations, such as teachers meeting students in their home, the IRS has held that such meetings are not the equivalent of meeting with customers, clients, or patients. We suppose that the IRS's reasoning is that, normally, students don't pay their teachers, if they pay anything at all. On the other hand, teachers who have private (paying) students in their home (such as

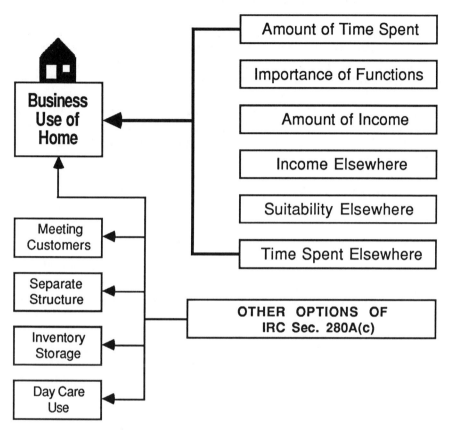

**Fig. 4.1 - "Testing Factors" for Principal Place of Business**

for private music lessons, dance lessons, language lessons) would qualify for the meeting test.

Regulation 1.280A-2(c) adds another interpretive twist. The meeting test alternate is fulfilled—

> *... only if the use of the dwelling unit by patients, clients, or customers is substantial and integral to the conduct of the business. Occasional meetings are insufficient.*

## Use of Separate Structure

Section 280A(c)(1)(C) provides a third alternative to (A) and (B) above. This is the "separate structure" test where the separate structure is used *in connection with* your trade or business. The implication here is that said structure need not be your principal place of business, nor your place of regularly meeting with customers. It is sufficient only that there be a separate business-use structure somewhere on the premises of your residence.

Regulation 1.280A-2(d) amplifies this concept by requiring that the structure be—

*Appurtenant to, but not attached to, the dwelling unit and is used exclusively and on a regular basis in connection with the taxpayer's trade or business. An artist's studio, a florist's greenhouse, and a carpenter's workshop are examples of structures that may be* [acceptable].

Elsewhere, the term "appurtenant to" has been defined as belonging to, accessory to, or incident to, the taxpayer's dwelling, but which is not attached to it.

To illustrate qualifying under alternative (C), suppose you own and operate a small floral shop in the business district of your residential area. Behind your home is a greenhouse where you grow plants and flowers, and then sell them in your shop. Although you also buy similar items from other growers, you do use your greenhouse regularly in connection with your floral business. All expenses for operating and maintaining your greenhouse would be deductible against your floral business income.

Similar qualifying examples would include dental technicians (who have a separate dental lab on their home property), mechanics, machinists, sign painters, and so on, who work in a converted garage structure that is detached from their house. Furthermore, the fact that the separate structure may have toilet, light cooking, and temporary sleeping facilities does not disqualify it as business property. That is, so long as the dwelling-like facilities are not used regularly for personal and family purposes.

## Storage of Inventory

If none of the above situations is applicable to your business use of home, there is one other option that could be applicable. This is the inventory storage rule of Section 280A(c)(2). It addresses those trades or businesses where the selling of inventory is a substantial element of the income production.

The storage rule [paragraph (2) of Sec. 280A(c)] reads in full as—

*Subsection (a)* [relating to "no deduction allowed"] *shall not apply to any item to the extent such item is allocable to space within the dwelling unit which is used on a regular basis as a storage unit for the inventory of the taxpayer held for use in the taxpayer's trade or business of selling products at retail or wholesale, but only if the dwelling unit is the sole fixed location of such trade or business.*

This provision is to enable "direct sellers" who have no other fixed outlets of their own, to use their home as their business address while they travel about making customer contacts and sales. These are persons who sell on a straight commission basis, and who are generally classed as representatives, consultants, distributors, and the like. Otherwise, without this storage rule, these self-employeds would be treated as itinerant tradesmen with no fixed place of business. As such, they would be denied all place-of-business deductions.

Depending on the nature, physical size, and quantity of products sold, the amount of inventory stored at home may be much less than the amount of inventory represented by actual gross sales. The rule is not intended to require direct sellers to convert their home into a bulk-storage warehouse. Thus, typically, the storage at home may consist of product samples, catalogs of products, initial order quantities, and material and supplies for packaging and shipping the initial orders.

The basic requirement for deductibility of storage-at-home expenses is that a specific area be so designated. This could be space in a garage, basement, attic, or utility room. The qualifying portion is only that amount of space which is actually used . . . and regularly so. It does not include empty space that might be adjacent to the storage space.

## Day Care Services

Paragraph (4) of Section 280A(c) sets up a special rule when using a portion of one's home for providing day care services.

These are custodial services provided to children, elderly persons, and those who are physically or mentally disabled. The day care rule is "special" in that it bypasses the exclusivity test that applies to all other business uses of your home. In other words, mixed use — personal, family, as well as business — is permitted.

The general rule on point [Sec. 280A(c)(4)(A)] reads in pertinent part as—

> *Subsection (a)* [relating to "no deduction allowed "] *shall not apply . . . to the use of any portion of the dwelling unit on a regular basis in the taxpayer's trade or busines of providing day care for children, for individuals who have attained age 65, or for individuals who are physically or mentally incapable of caring for themselves.*

Note that regular use is required, but not the exclusivity of use. However, an additional requirement is imposed. The owner or operator of the day care services at home must have applied for, been granted, or be exempt from—

> *A license certification, registration, or approval as a day care center or as a family or group day care home under the provisions of any applicable State law.*

Regulation 1.280A-2(f)(2) defines day care services as—

> [Those] *services which are primarily custodial in nature and which, unlike foster care, are provided for only certain hours during the day.* [They] *may include educational, developmental, or enrichment activities which are incidental to the primary custodial services. If the services performed in the home are primarily educational or instructional in nature, they do not qualify as day care services.*

There is still a further requirement: the *hours of use.* Since exclusivity of use is not required, the hours of regular use must be carefully documented. That is, the number of hours of day care use per day, times the number of days of day care use per year, gives the total use hours for the year. This number of hours, when divided by 8,760 hours in a year (365 days x 24 hours) gives the fraction of business use of that portion of the home which is used for day care services. The allocable portion of the home may include the entire dwelling unit (toilet, eating, sleeping, playing facilities) if need be.

## Business Use Percentage

Regardless of the type of business activity conducted in or out of your home, the portion allocable to such use must be established with specificity. The designated portion(s) must be identified as some fixed percentage of the total dwelling unit space. For this, *measured square footage* becomes the yardstick for tax accountability. Guessing and off-the-cuff estimates are not acceptable.

Regulation 1.280A-2(i)(3) addresses the business use of home percentage as follows:

*The taxpayer may determine the expenses allocable to the portion of the [dwelling] unit used for business purposes by any method that is reasonable under the circumstances. If the rooms in the dwelling unit are of approximately equal size, the taxpayer may ordinarily allocate the general expenses for the unit according to the number of rooms used for the business purpose. The taxpayer may also allocate general expenses according to the **percentage of the total floor space** in the unit that is used for the business purpose.* [Emphasis added.]

The best specificity approach is to simply get a tape measure, and measure the outside dimensions (length and breadth) of the partitions or walls that separate the business space of use. So long as there is a bona fide regular and exclusive use of the designated space, measure it. This includes garage areas, toilet areas, hallway areas, waiting room areas . . . whatever is used as appropriate to your business. But, be realistic.

Except for day care services, you must exclude the eating, sleeping, and recreational areas of your home. You can't deduct a portion of your bedroom even if you have a desk there that you occasionally use for business. The same applies to your kitchen. If you serve your customers coffee, tea, or snacks, occasionally, you can't write off a portion of your kitchen. The same also applies to your TV and family room, even though you may keep a few toys to entertain your client's children when doing business with their parent(s) in your home. Use some common sense.

We highly recommend that you prepare a not-to-scale drawing (plan view) of your home. Shade or emphasize the areas that are used for business. Show the dimensions of these areas in feet and inches. Also show the overall dimensions (total area) of your home. Multiply the length and breadth of each area to establish the square footage of that area. If there is more than one floor to your home, measure the area on each floor where there is business use.

As an illustration of what we are getting at, we present Figure 4.2. If you can present a sketch of your own home, either attached to your tax return, or at audit, along the lines illustrated, you have a better-than-average chance of your square footages being readily accepted.

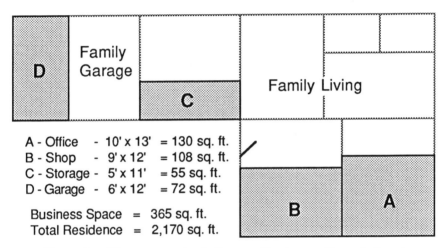

A - Office    - 10' x 13'  = 130 sq. ft.
B - Shop      - 9' x 12'   = 108 sq. ft.
C - Storage - 5' x 11'    = 55 sq. ft.
D - Garage  - 6' x 12'    = 72 sq. ft.

Business Space  =  365 sq. ft.
Total Residence  =  2,170 sq. ft.

**Fig. 4.2 - Measurement of Space: Business Use of Home**

We have just one cautionary note. If your business use percentage comes out to be less than 5%, we suggest that you **not** claim the business use deduction. On the other hand, if your percentage comes out to be more than 30%, prepare yourself for IRS challenge.

If you have a separate business structure on your residential premises, do **not** include that structure in the Figure 4.2 measurements. Such a structure requires a separate costing and expense analysis of its own.

## List of Deductible Expenses

Once you have established the specific business use percentage of your home, you are entitled to deduct certain expenses necessary for operating and maintaining your home. Accordingly, the following is a list of the types of expenses that are allowable:

| | | |
|---|---|---|
| *Priority I*: | ☐ | real estate taxes |
| (Class I) | ☐ | acquisition mortgage interest |
| | ☐ | casualty losses |

| | | |
|---|---|---|
| *Priority II*: | ☐ | equity mortgage interest |
| (Class II) | ☐ | home insurance |
| | ☐ | repairs and maintenance |
| | ☐ | phone and utilities |
| | ☐ | other expenses [such as rent (if a non-homeowner), security services, lawn care (if important to your customers), magazines (if in your waiting room), etc.] |

| | | |
|---|---|---|
| *Priority III* | ☐ | depreciation (of the building structure) |
| (Class III) | | |

The three priority groupings are because Section 280A(c)(5) — previously referred to as "paragraph (5)" — sets a limit on the overall amount of expenses that can be deducted. We won't quote the statutory wording on this point, as it is *very* confusing. Its essence is that your business use of home expenses cannot produce a net loss to the business.

The Priority I expenses are those items that you would be allowed, irrespective of whether your home is used for business or not. Priority II expenses are typically the kind you would not be allowed, if your home were not used for business. Even when used as a business, Priority II expenses are not allowed if your other not-home expenses produced a business loss. Priority III, depreciation expense, will depend on the amount of business profit remaining, if any, after the Priority II expenses are deducted.

## Form 8829: Overview

If you make business use of your home, and want to claim the expenses therewith, how do you do it?

As you may already suspect, there is a very special tax form for doing so. It is Form 8829: *Expenses for Business Use of Your Home*. It consists of some 50 lines for entering dollars and percentages. It is arranged in four separate parts with selected official instructions on its reverse side.

For introductory familiarization, we present an overview of Form 8829 in Figure 4.3. At this point, we simply want you to be aware of its general arrangement and what entry information is expected of you. If the form is pertinent to your modus operandi, by all means get the latest official copy of the form in your own hands. Obviously, we are not going to run down the form, line-by-line, here.

As you can see in Figure 4.3, Part I of Form 8829 is subtitled: *Area of Home Used for Business*. This is the business-use percentage that we covered earlier. You must enter your business-use square footage, and in the case of day care services, the total hours of day care use. You'll need a fixed percentage figure when doing Part II.

Part II is subtitled: *Figuring the Allowable Deduction*. This is the main body of the form, where most complications come in. The idea behind Part II is to limit your allowable deductions in a way that does not cause your overall business net earnings to be negative. Particularly note in Figure 4.3 that we have subarranged the expense entries into their three priority classes. The official form does not identify this subarrangement.

Part III of Form 8829 is subtitled: *Depreciation Allowable*. We have not discussed this item to any appreciable extent at this point. This is because there is another percentage that has to be introduced. There is also a question about depreciation of that separate structure, if any, on your premises. We'll cover the subject of depreciation more thoroughly in Chapter 7: Depreciation, Etc.

Part IV is subtitled: *Carryover of Unallowed Expenses*. This part tells you that if some or all of your deductible expenses and depreciation in Part II cannot be used currently, due to the limitation rules of Section 280A(c)(5), the unallowed portion can be carried over to the following year. You can keep carrying over your unallowed expenses year after year, so long as you are actively self-employed. In reality, if you are making a respectable livelihood in

| Form 8829 | EXPENSES FOR BUSINESS USE OF HOME | | Year |
|---|---|---|---|

| Name of Proprietor:_____ | Soc. Sec. Number |
|---|---|

**Part I**    **Area of Home Used for Business**

| Square footage for calculating your business use percentage | % [ ] |
|---|---|

**Part II**    **Figuring the Allowable Deduction**

Computational Base: Tentative Profit or Loss: Sch. C   [ ]

| Expense Items | (a) | (b) | |
|---|---|---|---|
| **Class I** | | | |
| **Class II** | | | |
| **Class III** | | | |
| | Allowable Expenses | | [ ] |

**Part III**    **Depreciation Allowable**

| See Chapter 7 herein | [ ] |
|---|---|

**Part IV**    **Carryover of Unallowed Expenses**

| Follow instructions on official form | [ ] |
|---|---|

**Fig. 4.3 - Form 8829 Generalized for Instructional Introduction**

your trade or business, your only carryovers would be those occurring in your loss year(s).

## Direct vs. Indirect Expenses

If you take another glance at Part II of Figure 4.3, you'll see that there are two columns (a) and (b). We have lifted these two columns from Figure 4.3 and expanded them in Figure 4.4. We also show in Figure 4.4 the line item designations that appear on the official form. Note that column (a) is headed: Direct expenses; column (b) is headed: Indirect expenses. The logical question is: What is the difference?

| Portion of Part II : FORM 8829 | | | |
|---|---|---|---|
| Tentative Profit or Loss from Schedule C | Computational Base ➤ | | [       ] |
| Expense Items | (a) Direct Expenses | (b) Indirect Expenses | |
| ☐ Casualty losses | | | |
| ☐ Mortgage interest  I | | | |
| ☐ Real estate taxes | | | |
| | | | |
| ● Mortgage interest  II | | | |
| ● Insurance | | | |
| ● Repairs & maint. | | | |
| ● Utilities | | | |
| ● Other expenses | | | |
| | | | |
| ◇ Carryover of prior year unalloweds | | | |
| See Official Form for Instructions | | | [       ] |

Fig. 4.4 - Allowable Home Deductions: Direct and Indirect

The official instructions on the back of Form 8829 are helpful in making the distinction, but not comprehensively so. The leadoff instruction to Part II reads—

*Enter as direct or indirect expenses only expenses for the business use of your home (i.e., expenses allowable only because your home is used for business). Other expenses, such as salaries, supplies, and business telephone, **which are deductible elsewhere** on [your return], should not be entered on Form 8829.* [Emphasis added.]

This instruction is trying to tell you that your business-only business expenses are deductible elsewhere on your return without regard to the limitation rule of Section 280A(c)(5). The whole purpose of Form 8829 is to confine and limit your business-use-of-home deductions. Secretly, we suspect that the IRS would like to discourage you from claiming any business home deductions.

Of those business expenses attributable directly to the use of your home, the Part II instruction tells you that—

*Direct expenses benefit only the business part of your home. They include painting or repairs made to the specific area or room used for business. Enter 100% of your direct expenses on the appropriate line in column (a).*

The instructions continue by telling you that—

*Indirect expenses are for keeping up and running your entire home. They benefit both the business and personal parts of your home. Generally, enter 100% of your indirect expenses on the appropriate expense line in column (b).*

The instructions are unclear as to whether you can make simultaneous entries in columns (a) and (b) for the same type of expense. The implication is that if there is an entry in column (a), column (b) is to be left blank. And, conversely, if there is an entry in column (b), column (a) is to be left blank. Yet, we can envision where both columns (for the same expense) could apply. This is particularly true where you have a separate structure on your premises, such as a lab or shop, while also using an office in the home. A point to note is that all entries in column (b) are multiplied by your business use percentage from Part I, whereas the entries in column (a) are **not** multiplied by said percentage.

## The Telephone Problem

Nothing is more direct/indirect confusing than using a telephone at home for business and, occasionally perhaps, for personal purposes, too. In any business these days, a telephone is ordinary and necessary. Also, connected to the phone line may be a fax machine and/or a computer modem. The telephone number is displayed on the business card and also on the business letterhead. Now, here's where the problem arises.

Tax Code Section 262(b): Treatment of Certain Phone Expenses, says—

*For purposes of* [disallowing any expense for personal, living, or family use], *in the case of an individual, any charge (including taxes thereon) for* **basic telephone service** *with respect to the 1st telephone line provided to any residence of the taxpayer shall be treated as a personal expense.* [Emphasis added.]

IRS officials interpret this rule to mean that no matter how little personal use is made of your business-in-home phone, the base charge is treated as a personal expense. This forces a self-employed to install two separate phone lines, even though one line may be fully adequate. This illustrates how tax laws can force your business expenses to be higher than they need be.

With only one phone line to your residence, many IRS auditors will require you to produce all phone bills for the taxable year. Then you are instructed to go down every listed phone call — some 1,000 to 3,000 typically in a business — and designate which are business and which are personal. This is a ridiculous way to administer the tax laws. One would think that the IRS would have more important things to do than harassing self-employed individuals concerning their phone calls. The IRS does not do this for large business establishments, even though it is well known that personal phone calls are made often from such businesses.

All of this phone call identification for a single line in a home could be eliminated if the rule of reason were applied. If, for example, it can be shown by other evidence that the phone is used predominantly for business, it should be accepted as such. The term "other evidence" could be the absence of teenage children at home, or that one's spouse is the primary business phone answerer. The term "predominantly" could mean 90% or more use of the phone for business purposes.

What we are trying to illustrate here is that business use of the home can raise some pesky, picky issues when it comes to applying certain tax laws.

### File With Schedule C

Immediately below the official title on Form 8829, there is a bold lettered instruction which reads:

▶ *File with Schedule C (Form 1040)*

(Schedule C, incidentally, is titled: Profit or Loss from Business.) Below this instruction is another which reads:

▶ *See instructions on back.*

The instructions on the back of Form 8829 make it pretty clear that Form 8829 is strictly an appendage to Schedule C. That is, Schedule C is the primary place for entering one's business expenses. In particular, the instructions say—

*Other expenses . . . which are deductible elsewhere on Schedule C, should not be entered on Form 8829.*

This instruction is trying to caution you against making a duplicate entry of the same expense item on both tax forms. If it is on Form 8829, it should not be on Schedule C. And vice versa.

In the expenses portion of Schedule C, there are a number of line items which duplicate those on Form 8829. Examples are: mortgage interest, insurance, repairs, utilities, depreciation, and others. Because of this duplication, a headnote to the expenses portion of Schedule C reads—

**Caution**: *Enter expenses for business use of your home on* **Form 8829**.

This cautionary note affirms the hand-and-glove relationship between Schedule C and Form 8829. The relationship is furthered by a summary line on Form 8829 which says—

*Allowable expenses for business use of your home. Enter here and on Schedule C.*

Then, on Schedule C, there is a corresponding line which says—

*Expenses for business use of your home (attach Form 8829).*

Because of the importance of the Schedule C-Form 8829 relationship, we diagram it for you in Figure 4.5. We particularly want you to note that your business-use-of-home expenses are

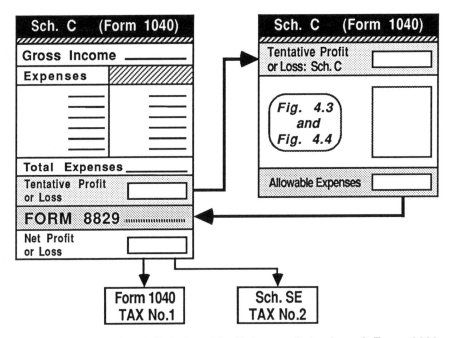

Fig. 4.5 - Procedural Relationship Between Sch. C and Form 8829

deducted **after** a *tentative* profit or loss has been established. If you have a net loss after the allowable expenses on Form 8829 are subtracted, you have to checkbox one of two at-risk investment questions. We'll get to at-risk and other matters on Schedule C in Chapter 9: Net Profit or Loss.

# 5

# DIRECT COST ITEMS

---

**Between Gross Receipts And Gross Profit, There Are Special Subtractions For DIRECT COSTS. These Are Priority Items Known As "Returns And Allowances" And "Cost Of Goods Sold." Determining Cost of Goods Sold Is An 8-Step Computational Process Of Its Own. Your ENDING INVENTORY Becomes Tied-Up Money Which Is Income Taxed. Valuing And Paying For Direct Costs Can Pose Year-End Accounting Problems. However, IRC Sections 446 And 471 Allow You To Use Common Sense Methods, Such As "Cash Is 30 Days Net," If Applied Consistently Year After Year.**

---

This chapter will have special meaning for you if the nature of your business is such that you are engaged in—

(a) the production of real or tangible personal property for sale to customers, or
(b) the acquisition of real or tangible personal property for resale to customers,

This is because you enter a whole new world of direct cost accounting. In 1986, Section 263A: Capitalization and Inclusion in Inventory Costs of Certain Expenses, was added to the Internal Revenue Code. This new law and its regulations thereunder comprise more than 35,000 words of tax text.

Fortunately, much of Section 263A — especially the acquisition for resale rules — do not apply to small-business owners. As per subsection 263A(b)(2)(B), a "small business" is an activity where the gross receipts for the taxable year do not exceed $10,000,000 (10 million). Not many self-owned proprietorships generate this kind of gross receipts. However, all of the "production for sale" rules apply, regardless of the business gross receipts. Small businesses are particularly affected when they produce (for sale) tangible personal property.

Subsection 263A(b), very last sentence, defines "tangible personal property" as including—

*...film, sound recording, video tape, book or similar property.*

The term "similar property" includes computer programs, technical reports, poster signs, artist paintings, printed circuits, and so on. These are the kinds of things many self-employed businesses do. When they do, accounting for the *direct costs* (parts, materials, labor, etc.) becomes a prime target for the IRS's revenue enhancement program.

By forcing a taxpayer to classify certain costs and expenditures as "direct," the IRS can automatically tie up that money — AND TAX IT — until the goods and products are either sold or destroyed. We touched on this matter in Chapter 3: Keeping Proper Records, but we want to expand on it here.

## "Direct Costs" Defined

The tax accounting starting point for any self-employment business is: *Gross receipts or sales.* This is the term used whether the business is a sole proprietorship (Schedule C: Form 1040) or a general partnership (Schedule A: Form 1065). From the gross receipts, the direct cost items are subtracted, to arrive at the *gross profit* for the business. From the gross profit, other operating expenses are deducted to arrive at net profit or loss (for a proprietorship) or ordinary income or loss (for a partnership). Because of the similarity of direct cost accounting in proprietorship and partnership businesses, we'll dwell primarily on proprietorship (Schedule C) matters. The Schedule C sequence: Profit or Loss from Business, is basic to all self-employment forms.

All direct cost accounting takes place between gross sales and gross profit. The costs are "direct" in the sense that they are expenditures for merchandise, parts, materials, labor, and other items (permits, freight) that become the products or services that **go**

**directly to** your customers. These are "costs" in the sense that, generally, you have to pay for them in advance of your selling them. Thus, your direct costs become your very first order of subtraction against your gross receipts.

All of which means that you want to spend adequate time for establishing — and substantiating — your direct costs for the year. These are your "off the top" costs. If you have paid your direct cost bills, sooner or later you will be allowed full subtractions for them.

If the IRS can minimize your direct cost subtractions, it can automatically force an increase in your gross profit. This, in turn, means increased tax revenues. This also means that you have spent up-front money for which you derive no tax benefit.

Your direct costs are separated into two distinct subtraction categories. These are: (a) Returns and allowances, and (b) Cost of goods sold. The simple sequence procedure is this—

Gross Receipts or Sales
LESS Returns and allowances
LESS Cost of goods sold
EQUALS: Gross Profit

Actually, direct cost accounting is more involved than this simple sequence suggests. There are at least four major stages, as depicted in Figure 5.1. The "cost of goods sold" (stage 4) is primarily where the IRS points its big guns to drive the subtractional amounts down.

The key to the cost-of-goods subtraction is ending inventory (stage 3). The lower this ending inventory, the higher the cost of goods sold (relative to actual costs expended). The higher the cost of goods sold, the lower the gross profit. The lower the gross profit, the lower the tax revenue to government. This is why, as you'll see below, the IRS focuses on ending inventory for maximizing its tax take.

## Returns and Allowances

"Gross receipts or sales" comprises all monetary payments that you receive from your customers, clients, or patients. Said payments include deposits, advances, prepayments, full payments, and late payments. All of these derive directly from the goods, products, or services that you render to your clientele. Presumably, all of these payments go directly into your business bank account.

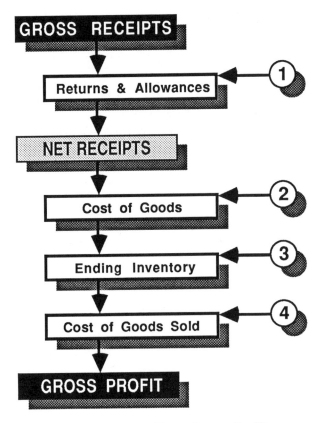

Fig. 5.1 - Key Stages in Figuring Your Gross Profit

In every business, there arise situations, after money is received, when some — sometimes, all — of it has to be returned or refunded. In some cases, allowances and reimbursements have to be made for errors, misunderstandings, and defects. It is from this reality of business that the subtraction of *returns and allowances* is validated.

The term *returns* includes all forms of rebates, refunds, and adjustments where money is returned, in full or partially, directly to a customer. A typical example is where a customer pays $150 for an item. He is dissatisfied with the item and returns it to you. You refund his $150 in full. In the meantime, you had deposited the $150 in your bank. There, it will show up in your gross receipts.

When you pay the money back, you want it to show up as a subtraction from your gross receipts.

Another classical example is a bounced check. A client pays you $200 by personal check. You deposit it in the bank. A week or two later, it comes back to you stamped: "Insufficient Funds." Simultaneously, the bank debits your account for $205. Now, you have a $205 subtraction from your gross receipts.

The term *allowances* includes adjustments and discounts for overcharges, defects, and damages endured by customers. It also includes reimbursement to a customer for money he paid to someone else to correct or repair the product or service he acquired from you. Collectively, this is called "pain and suffering" money that you have to pay to customers to make amends either for your misdeeds or for imperfections in your product or service.

We are trying to emphasize a basic point. That is, "returns and allowances" comprise all those monies that you give back directly to your customers. You receive money from them; you give money back; you are entitled to a subtraction from your gross receipts.

Whether you receive the money in one year, and pay it back the next year, doesn't really matter. When you actually pay it back, it becomes a direct cost item of subtraction.

## Sales Tax, If Included

Another item of direct subtraction is your collection of state and local sales tax. If you collect sales tax from your customers and the amount is included in your bank deposits and gross receipts, the amount of said tax is a direct cost subtraction. Otherwise, you could wind up paying income tax (both No. 1 and No. 2) on your sales tax collections.

Where sales tax is imposed, and it applies to your products or services, you are automatically deputized as a *sales tax collector*. You get neither pay nor thanks for this, of course. You not only have to collect the proper amount of tax from your customers, you have to account periodically to a designated sales tax agency. For this, Sales Tax Returns are required (monthly, quarterly, or annually). When the due date of sales tax returns comes up, you have to immediately turn in the tax monies collected.

Certainly, you need to keep some record of your taxable sales and services, for preparing your sales tax returns. But we don't see any point in trying to separate the sales tax proceeds from your gross receipts, when you make deposits in your bank.

There is a better way. Take your sales tax returns for the year, total the amount of tax payments you made to the sales tax agency, and subtract this total directly from your bank-deposited gross receipts. As long as you do this consistently year after year, the IRS will accept this subtraction as a direct cost item.

The question arises: How do you show this subtraction on your Schedule C (Form 1040)?

Answer: The sales tax that you collected and paid out is a variant of your "returns and allowances." The only difference is that it is paid to your sales tax agency, and not to your customers. The tax money is collected from your customers, but it goes to a tax authority. This is not money that properly becomes part of your gross profit.

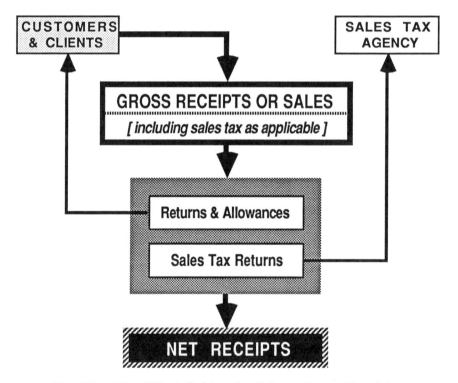

**Fig. 5.2 - The "First Subtraction" from Gross Receipts**

Your profit or loss form (Schedule C) has a subtractive line designated as: Returns and allowances. Simply hand-print or typewrite on the same line the words: "and sales tax." Upon doing this, the printed line will now read as:

*Returns and allowances, and sales tax.*

You then subtract this total from your Schedule C gross receipts for the year, to arrive at your net receipts. This is your "first subtraction" from gross receipts and is depicted in Figure 5.2.

## Cost of Goods Sold

Your "second subtraction" from gross receipts/sales is cost of goods sold. This is an 8-step sequence which includes a major subtraction step of its own. This subtraction step is: *ending inventory*. But, before you can determine your ending inventory, there are five major steps to account your way through.

The cost-of-goods-sold sequence is presented in Figure 5.3. We have edited the official wording slightly, and have sequenced the line numbers consecutively. The tax form wording and line numbers differ depending on whether a proprietorship or partnership is involved. We have generalized Figure 5.3 to apply to either form of business.

The Figure 5.3 sequence appears on proprietorship tax returns as Part III, Schedule C, Form 1040. The same sequence appears on a partnership tax return as Schedule A, Form 1065. The same official heading: Cost of Goods Sold, is used on both returns.

We wish to call your attention now to Steps 1 and 7 in Figure 5.3. Step 1 is: Inventory, beginning; Step 7 is: Inventory, ending. The "beginning/ending," of course, refers to beginning of year and ending of year. Inventory at beginning of year is simply the closing inventory of the preceding year. If there is any difference in the two entry amounts, an explanation is required. The official instructions at Step 1 say—

*If different from last year's closing inventory, attach explanation.*

Explanation of the ending/beginning difference may be a short annotation hand-entered on the official form, or it may be a separate attachment giving full details. Typical explanations include: corrective adjustments; differences between physical inventory and

| | | |
|---|---|---|
| 1. | Inventory, beginning ............................................... | $ _____ |
| 2. | Purchases for resale ........................................... (less personal withdrawals) | _____ |
| 3. | Cost of labor ................................................ (exclusive of your own) | _____ |
| 4. | Materials and supplies ....................................... | _____ |
| 5. | Other costs  (explain) ....................................... | _____ |
| 6. | TOTAL  (Add steps 1 thru 5)............................... | _____ |
| 7. | Inventory, ending ............................................ | _____ |
| 8. | COST OF GOODS SOLD............................... (subtract step 7 from step 6) | [ ] |

Fig. 5.3 - Computation Sequence: Cost of Goods Sold

computed inventory; culling and discarding damaged items; or change in valuation method(s).

## Purchases for Resale

Step 2 in the cost-of-goods sequence is: Purchases for resale. This is your cost of goods and merchandise that you buy and hold for resale to customers and clients. The entry amount consists of your total purchases for the taxable year, at whatever discount price you actually pay. Whether you pay cash on delivery or "30 days net," your true cost constitutes your purchase cost.

When you purchase items for resale, most state laws require that you obtain a *Resale Permit* from the state agency having jurisdiction over sales tax matters. This permit enables you to make your bulk purchases without paying all sales tax out of your own pocket. For this privilege, you are required to collect the sales tax from the pockets of your customers and clients. This was the collection and payover scheme shown in Figure 5.2.

On sales tax matters, we urge that you contact the local office of your state sales taxing agency. When making inquiry, be prepared to be inundated with regulatory directives and specialized tax forms. Take particular care not to overestimate your anticipated sales for the year. Otherwise, you'll be required to make a substantial up-front deposit of the first year's sales tax revenues — out of your own pocket. This deposit is held in an escrow account, as insurance against any delinquent sales tax returns. It may be returned to you after **five years**, if you insist. In the meantime, your sales tax deposit is NOT one of your direct cost items. It is an insurance impound which is fully refundable, if all conditions are met.

Independent of sales tax matters, the small-print instructions at Step 2 (of Figure 5.3), require you to subtract—

*Cost of items withdrawn for personal use.*

This purchase subtraction is of significance particularly when selling food and beverage, clothing and apparel, household furnishings, recreational items, and the like.

Other than minor repairs and packaging for shipping, purchases for resale imply very little fabrication work on your part. It could well be that purchasing for resale comprises the main cost-of-goods-sold activity of your business.

## Labor and Other Costs

When you design, manufacture, and ship products to your customers and clients, or purchase parts which you rework and install on their vehicles, equipment, or premises, you become a "producer of goods." This is different from being a purchaser for resale. As the producer, you may sell your products at wholesale (to others who resell them) or at retail (direct to the end user). Either way, you are concerned with an important direct cost item classed as *direct labor*.

Your direct labor costs appear in two places in Figure 5.3. They appear at Step 3 (Cost of labor) and/or at Step 5 (Other costs). There is a clear tax distinction between these two steps. Step 3 pertains to *employee* labor, whereas Step 5 pertains to *nonemployee* labor. If you make an entry at Step 3, the IRS will be looking for Forms W-2 (Wage and Tax Statement). If you make an entry at Step 5, the IRS will be looking for Forms 1099-MISC

(Miscellaneous Income). These are payer reporting forms that you need as backup documentation.

If you have no employees — that is, if you are not withholding social security, medicare, and income taxes (federal, state, local) — MAKE NO ENTRY at Step 3. Any entry here signals the IRS that you are an employer. As such, a whole new world of tax, reporting, and withholding demands is imposed upon you.

Many self-employed small business owners "get by" by engaging nonemployee direct labor. They do this by farming out most of the work to others. They engage one or more of the following types of contractors—

A. *Outside contractors* — shop owners who themselves have the fabrication equipment, machinery, and personnel to produce the products (or principal portions thereof) that you want.

B. *Independent contractors* — persons who, using their own tools and equipment, do the final fabrication and installation (of your products) to your specifications; they do this on a job-by-job basis.

C. *Rental contractors* — persons who rent your shop space and equipment from you, and produce the products or services that you want, but who are also free to produce similar products and services for others.

Whatever you do for Steps 3 and 5, do **not** include your own design/production/fabrication/installation labor. Your compensation, whatever it might be, is the net profit or loss from your business overall.

Included in "other costs" (Step 5) are such items as freight, permits, inspections, rework costs, and whatever else is necessary to produce, prepare, and get your product or service to your customers satisfactorily.

## Materials and Supplies

Step 4 (in Figure 5.3) is a catchall direct cost item for those materials and supplies that go into your end product. The line entry on your cost-of-goods-sold schedule includes raw materials, finished or semi-finished parts, solvents, paints, cleaning rags, cardboard boxes, welding supplies, hand tools, saw blades, and myriads of other necessities that you buy from others for manufacturing, storing, and shipping your end products or services to customers. Thus, these items are those that are directly part of the product or service that you deliver.

Part of the cost of these items is the cost of hauling away and dumping your scrap materials, hazardous wastes, and recyclable items. In environmentally sensitive areas, the disposal costs alone can be substantial.

All of these miscellaneous direct cost items are classed as *shop supplies*. Here the term "shop" is used to distinguish the production side of your business from the administrative side. Administratively, you also use "office supplies." But these two classes of supplies are tax treated differently. Shop supplies are capitalized, whereas office supplies are expensed. Until your product or service is sold, your shop supplies wind up in your ending inventory. Included in said inventory are also those *unopened* boxes, crates, or containers of your shop materials and supplies.

Also included in ending inventory is any unfinished work in process that you may have. Until the product or service that you produce (or purchase for resale) has been actually "shipped out the door," all other of your direct costs become part of your closing inventory at the end of the year.

## Valuing Closing Inventory

Ideally, self-employed business owners would like to have ZERO closing inventory. This way, they would have no money tied up in unsold merchandise.

There are only three acceptable ways to do this, namely:

*One.* Limit your business to pure consulting and service-type activities where you have no cost of goods sold.

*Two.* Limit your cost of goods sold to
(a) purchases to order,
(b) productions to order, or
(c) preparations to order.

Here, made "to order" means that you purchase, produce, or prepare your offered products or services only after you have essentially presold them.

*Three.* Deliberately load up, haul away, and have all unsold inventory destroyed . . . and third-party certified as such.

In all other situations, you will have an end-of-the-year (closing) inventory of some kind. And you may have been carrying some of that inventory year after year. Thus, the tax question arises: How do you value your closing inventory?

This is where the little check-boxes on the cost-of-goods-sold tax schedules come in. A statement/question appears that asks:

*Method(s) used to value closing inventory—*

☐ *Cost*            ☐ *Lower of cost or market*
☐ *Write-down of subnormals*    ☐ *LIFO (last in, first out)*
☐ *Average cost*         ☐ *Other (attach explanation)*

Below these check-boxes (on the tax forms) you are asked:

*Was there any change in determining quantities, cost, or valuations between opening and closing inventory?* ☐ *Yes* ☐ *No. If "Yes," attach explanation.*

Before checking any of these valuation boxes, you should know what Section 471 of the IR Code says. It says, in part, that—

*Whenever . . . the use of inventories is necessary in order clearly to determine the income of any taxpayer, inventories shall be taken by such taxpayer on such basis . . . as conforming as nearly as may be to the **best accounting practice** in the trade or business and as most clearly reflecting the income.* [Emphasis added.]

In other words, you can use whatever inventory valuation method that conforms to the "best accounting practice" in your trade or business. For self-employeds, this is the *cost* or *average cost* method which can be substantiated with paid supplier invoices.

Otherwise, if you try to use more sophisticated methods, the IRS will come up with its bizarre theories for maximizing the total value of your closing inventory.

## Year-End Accounting

Valuing ending/closing inventory raises questions about accounting methods used for gross receipts and cost of goods at end of the year. For example, you sold and billed a customer for goods and services, but come December 31, he has not paid you. Is this a gross receipts entry for the December ending year? On the outgo (disbursement) side, suppose you ordered and received goods from a supplier in December, but didn't pay him until January. Does this direct cost item go into your December ending year? Or, does it go into your January beginning year accounting?

The answer to these questions depends on your method of year-end accounting: *cash* or *accrual*, or some *hybrid* of the two. You are allowed to choose any method that you want, so long as you do so regularly and consistently year after year. The method you choose must also clearly reflect your proper income. On this point, Section 446(a): ***General Rule for Methods of Accounting***, says—

*Taxable income shall be computed under the method of accounting on the basis of which the taxpayer regularly computes his income in keeping his books.*

The cash method of accounting is the simplest and fairest for small businesses. Under the cash method, income is reported in the year that it is actually received. Under the accrual method, when you bill a customer for goods or services purchased, the billed amount is treated as constructively received in the year billed. If the billing is in December, and the customer doesn't pay until several months later, you pay tax on the billed amount in the December ending year. This just does not make sense to a small business owner. It is for this reason that the cash method of *income* accounting is most preferred.

The same cash method concept also applies to disbursements. When you actually pay for an item, it is treated as such in the year paid. Under the accrual method, when you are billed for an item, it is treated as constructively paid in the year billed. If you use the cash method for income, you must also use it for outgo.

The cash versus accrual method creates inconsistencies when it comes to costing your ending inventory. You may have ordered some merchandise and materials which you actually received in December, but which you did not pay for until January or later. So, which method do you use for costing the received but unpaid inventory?

Most suppliers bill for goods shipped (to their long-established accounts) on a "30 days net" cash-type basis. And many suppliers offer a 1% to 3% discount, if the bill is paid within 10 days.

With this general business practice in mind, we suggest that all direct cost items billed in December, but paid in January, be counted in your December ending year. This 30-day grace period automatically precludes counting any January billings and any payments made after January 31. We want to stress that this 30-day accrual-cash hybrid applies ONLY TO your direct cost items (returns and allowances; sales tax returns; cost of goods, supplies, and services; and ending inventory). It does NOT apply to ordinary expense items.

## A Reminder

We cannot overstress the importance of your cost-of-goods-sold accounting (Figure 5.3 revisited). Nor can we overstress the importance of cash-basis discipline in paying your December-incurred bills before January 31. This way, your *direct costs* (only) are treated as December-ending-year items. The real challenge, of course, is to minimize your end-of-the-year inventory.

If you are in a purely consulting or purely service-type business, you may not have any cost-of-goods-sold accounting. But, you may have, without realizing it. You may have no ending inventory, but you probably have some direct costs, such as nonemployee compensation, outside vendors, technical reports, purchases of parts, materials and supplies, shipping, and other cost items which go to, or directly benefit, your customers and clients. If you do have such costs, you want to prioritize them by subtracting them before displaying gross profit on your tax return.

# 6

# EMPLOYEES vs. NONEMPLOYEES

It Is Possible, Though Difficult At Times, To Run A Business Solely With Nonemployees. Doing So Avoids Employee Payrolls, Employee Withholdings, Employer Matchings, Federal (And State) Tax Deposits, And The 100% LIABILITY PENALTY Therewith. For Employees, You Require Form W-4; For Nonemployees, Form W-9. For Employees, You Submit QUARTERLY Employer Tax Returns And Prepare Annually Forms W-2. For Nonemployees, Form 1099-MISC Only Is Required. To Counter IRS's Lust For Reclassifying Your Nonemployees, You Need To Familiarize Yourself With the SAFE HARBOR Rule of 1978.

It would be ideal, we suppose, that as a self-employed individual, you could carry on a lucrative trade or business, year after year, without having to pay compensation to anyone else for services in your behalf. That is, you do all the solicitation of business, all the planning and management, and all the work of getting your product or service to your customers and clients. If married, your spouse helps you as necessary. But other than you and your spouse, you pay no one else for any necessary service for running your business.

Perhaps this is the ideal, but we doubt that you could earn a comfortable living by doing so. There is only so much that one individual (married or not) can do. Sooner or later, "outside help" is required. When such help is engaged, a serious tax dilemma arises.

Do you engage your helpers as employees? Or, do you engage them as nonemployees?

There is a world of tax difference between employees and nonemployees. If you engage just one employee, you have all of the tax forms, paperwork, and withholding liability of any major U.S. corporation. If you have one or more nonemployees, your tax paperwork is much simplified. BUT, when you have one or more nonemployees, the IRS — and its counterpart state agencies — are on your back continually trying to force the reclassification of your nonemployees as employees. Employee reclassification is a vast source of untapped tax and penalty revenue for governments.

In this chapter, therefore, we want to focus on the re- classification controversy, and point out how unreasonable tax agencies can be. We also want to give you some guidelines on how you may engage nonemployees and have that status stick, even when tax challenged. The goal of all tax agencies, it seems, is that there shall be no nonemployees.

## Employer ID Number

If you are going to be self-employed on an ongoing basis, one of your early-on chores is to apply for an Employer Identification Number (EIN). For this, you need to obtain (from the IRS or from your tax advisor) *Form SS-4: Application for . . .* [EIN].

This application itself in no way ties your hands and commits you to having employees. A subheading on the form clearly says—

*For use by employees **and others**.* [Emphasis added.]

It is the "for others" part that you initially want an EIN.

Whether you have employees, nonemployees, or neither, an ongoing trade or business is legitimated by having a federal ID number. Often, your customers and clients, particularly if in a trade or business of their own, will need from you a TIN (Taxpayer Identification Number) for their own tax records and reportings. If you do not provide them with an EIN, you must provide them with your SSN (Social Security Number).

In this day and age of taxpayers reporting on taxpayers — to the IRS (and to state agencies) — an EIN or SSN is a computer requirement of life. When a tax ID is requested of you, and you resist, delay, or sidestep responding, you raise some doubts in the requester's mind. Are you legit, or not? Are you engaged in the "underground economy"? Most customers and clients, unless they themselves are in the underground economy, want no part of participating with you in such matters.

It is so much easier to apply for an EIN and provide that number to any of your clientele, when so requested.

When filling out Form SS-4, you want to read carefully the official instructions. They start on the back of the form itself. Particularly read the part where it says—

> *Who Must File. You must file this form if you have not obtained an EIN before and—*
> * *You pay wages to one or more employees.*
> * *You are required to have an EIN to use on any return, statement, or other document, even if you are not an employer.*
> * *You are required to withhold taxes on income, other than wages . . . .*
> *Individuals who file Schedule C (Form 1040) . . . must use EINs if they have a Keogh* [or SEP retirement] *plan or are required to file excise, employment, or alcohol, tobacco, or firearms returns.*

Thus, you see, even if you have no employees and never intend to have employees, you still need an EIN. So, don't fight it. Go do it. Get Form SS-4 and fill it out.

We offer only one precautionary note. It pertains to the question about midway down the form which reads—

> *Enter highest number of employees expected in the next 12 months. Note: If the applicant does not expect to have any employees during the period, enter "O".*

Even if you expect someday to have employees, still enter "O" at the SS-4 item above. You can *always* amend any tax statement to add employees. There is no need to commit yourself prematurely to having them. If you leave the space blank, the IRS will assume that you already have employees.

## Liability for Withholdings

Your most onerous task regarding employees is your liability for certain withholdings. This task is onerous, thankless, and punitive.

As an employer, you are required (mandated/commanded) to withhold, as applicable, federal income taxes, social security taxes, and medicare taxes. To these withholdings, you add from your business receipts the *employer-matching* part of social security and medicare. There is no point in our citing the tax code on this. Tax withholding is common knowledge among employers and employees.

What is not so common knowledge is that, as employer, you are responsible for withholding the correct amount, regularly each pay period. Additionally, you must safeguard the withholdings — and your matchings — in an entirely separate "tax account" of its own. Above all, you MUST NOT commingle the withholdings and matchings with your gross receipts of the business (as you can do with sales tax collections). Herein lies the greatest punitive liability for being an employer.

Federal tax withholdings (and counterpart state tax withholdings, too) are designated as **employee trust money**. This money does not belong to the employer, even temporarily. It is priority trust money which you must protect and periodically pay over. You must do this regardless of the condition of the national economy and regardless of the state of your business. Using this money for ordinary business transactions — even for one day — risks imposition of the 100% penalty.

On this penalty point, IRC Section 6672(a): *Failure to Collect and Pay Over Tax*, says—

> *Any person required to collect, truthfully account for, and pay over any tax imposed . . . who willfully fails to* [do so] *. . . shall, in addition to other penalties provided by law, be liable to a penalty* **equal to the total amount of the tax** *. . . not collected, or not accounted for and paid over.* [Emphasis added.]

The "equal to the total amount of the tax" is 100% of the withholdings . . . and matchings.

To whom do you pay over this tax? Do you pay it to the IRS?

No. You must deposit it with an authorized commercial bank using a special deposit form. This is **Form 8109**: Federal Tax Deposit Coupon. Generally, for withholdings and matchings totaling less than $3,000, the deposits are made by the 15th day of the following month. If more than $3,000, the deposits are required by the 3rd banking day after the close of the pay period.

Many a small business has been closed down and terminated by the IRS, for failure to collect, account for, and pay over the employee withholdings in a timely manner. Some self-employeds just don't seem to grasp the gravity of this situation. Even a glance at Figure 6.1 should impress on you the importance of withholdings, matchings, and payovers.

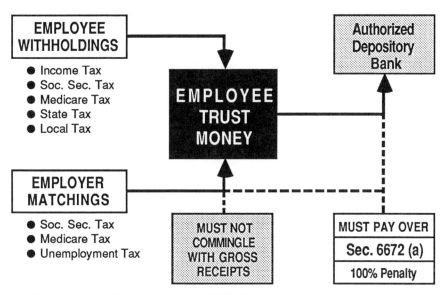

Fig. 6.1 - Employer "Always Liable" for Employee Trust Money

## Backup Withholding Limited

In sharp contrast to the above, if you engage nonemployees only, you face no general withholding requirements. This is because a nonemployee, supposedly, is in a separate trade or business of his or her own. As such, a nonemployee is responsible for his/her own taxes, including social security and medicare. Thus, no withholdings on your part also means that you are not required to contribute social security and medicare matchings.

In rare cases, as a nonemployer engaging nonemployees, you may be required to institute *backup withholding* on IRS-designated nonemployees. The amount of backup withholding is a flat 20% of any *reportable payment*. A "reportable payment" to a nonemployee is the amount of $600 or more for any calendar year [IRC Sec. 6041A(a)].

The authority for backup withholding is set forth in Tax Code Section 3406(a): ***Requirement to Deduct and Withhold***. In paraphrased form, withholding is required ONLY IF—

    (a)   the payee [the nonemployee] fails to provide you with his EIN or SSN;

    (b)   the payee provides you with an incorrect EIN or SSN, or

    (c)   the IRS notifies you that the payee has underreported his income to the IRS.

In other words, backup withholding does not apply across the board to all of your nonemployees. It applies only to designated nonemployees: those who do not provide their correct EIN or SSN, or who do not report all of their income to the IRS. The idea behind the 20% withholding is to put a dent in the underground economy, and to bring recalcitrant payees into line.

Even when the IRS instructs you to institute backup withholding, it applies only to the "reportable payment." No social security or medicare withholding and matching are involved. Just income tax withholding.

You can avoid backup withholding altogether. You do so by making sure that your nonemployees provide you with their correct (full) names, correct EIN or SSN, and some assurance that they have filed their own returns in a timely manner. We'll provide more instructions in this regard as we go along. If the IRS directs you to commence backup withholding on just one nonemployee, you face all of the liability and procedural requirements of Figure 6.1 for employees.

## Employee Form W-4

If you have ever been an employee yourself, you already know about Form W-4. It is titled: ***Employee's Withholding Allowance Certificate***. As an employer, you must require each of your prospective employees to complete Form W-4, preferably *before* commencing any work under your supervision.

The form requires the employee to enter not only his (or her) name and address, but also his social security number (SSN). It is the SSN that you want to be absolutely sure is correct. The only way to confirm this number is to request to see the prospective employee's actual/official Social Security card. Have him present it to you for photocopying, and attach the photocopy to his completed Form W-4. If he has no Social Security card, direct him to the Social Security Administration Office nearest to your place of business.

Before you allow any person to commence work for you as an employee, review the completed Form W-4 in said person's presence. Particularly make sure that one of the three check-boxes: ☐ *Single,* ☐ *Married,* or ☐ *Married, but withhold at higher Single rate,* is checked. You need this status information when selecting from the income tax withholding tables.

There are also four line entries (on Form W-4) that you should review carefully. These lines are—

- Number of withholding allowances claimed.
- Additional amounts, if any, to be deducted.
- Whether "Exempt" status is claimed.
- Whether the person is a full-time student.

Ordinarily, your submission of Forms W-4 to the IRS is not required. However, if a person claims more than 10 withholding allowances, you must submit that form to the IRS. When you do so, the IRS will automatically impose a $500 penalty on the claimant [Sec. 6682]. To remove this penalty, the employee must prove that he is entitled to a higher number than 10. For such proof, a pro forma (estimated) tax return for the entire year must be submitted to the IRS by the employee.

If a person claims "Exempt" from withholdings, you should review with the claimant the three conditions on Form W-4 that must be met. If a person claims exempt status willfully and fraudulently, he/she is subject to a $1,000 fine, up to one year imprisonment, or both [Sec. 7205].

The W-4 "Withholding Certificate" applies only to *income* tax withholdings. It has no effect — NONE WHATSOEVER — on social security and medicare withholdings. These withholdings and your matching contributions apply if a person earns so much as *10 cents* per pay period. This is absolutely true! For example, if an employee earns between 9 cents and 25 cents, his social security/medicare tax is the grand sum of 1 cent. Additionally, you have to contribute a matching 1 cent as the employer.

Once you have an employee, there is no escape from withholdings, no matter how little compensation you may pay.

### Nonemployee Form W-9

If you engage nonemployees, you still need a W-4-type form to submit to each such person. This is Form W-9: *Request for Taxpayer Identification Number and Certification.* The request is addressed to the payee (your nonemployee). You are requesting that he/she provide you with a correct SSN or EIN, and that he/she certify — *under penalties of perjury* — that the ID number provided is indeed correct.

The W-9 form is arranged into three separate blocks, namely:

Part I     — Taxpayer Identification Number
                • either SSN or EIN as appropriate
Part II    — Payees Exempt from Backup Withholding
                • employee-type services are seldom exempt
Part III   — Certification (under penalties of perjury)

There are ample self-guiding instructions on the front and back of the form. Among these instructions, the W-9 says—

☐   *If you fail to furnish your correct TIN [SSN or EIN] to a requester, you are subject to a penalty of $50 for each such failure.*

☐   *If you make a false statement . . . that results in no imposition of backup withholding, you are subject to a penalty of $500.*

☐   *Willfully falsifying certifications or affirmations may subject you to criminal . . . fines and/or imprisonment.*

Many nonemployers fail totally to take advantage of Form W-9. Instead, they make an informal oral request for the ID information. This leaves them without any documentation should the IRS notify them to commence backup withholding. Form W-9 carries the nonemployee's signed certification that—

*(1)   The number shown on this form is my correct taxpayer identification number . . ., and*

*(2)   I am not subject to backup withholding because: . . . (b) I have not been notified by the IRS that I am subject to backup withholding.*

The IRS issues its backup withholding notice to payers (nonemployers) via its computer printout form CP 2100. In its four-paragraphic directive, it states, in part, that—

*You* [the nonemployer] *may be liable for the amounts which you may have failed to withhold. . . . A payer is subject to the same requirements for failing to backup withhold as an employer who makes payments of wages.*

If you receive such a notice (CP 2100), it is a prelude to the IRS's seeking to reclassify your nonemployees as employees. Hence, you had better insist on a signed Form W-9 from each of your nonemployees, *before* the IRS comes at you.

### Payroll Paperwork

If you intend to have, or do have, one or more employees, prepare yourself for an extensive amount of paperwork. Foremost in this regard is a payroll ledger. You need to set up an accounting ledger for each employee. Don't put two or more employees on the same ledger (EVEN IF the two are husband and wife). Payroll accounting is a per employee (per individual) affair. If for no other reason, separate earnings accounting is required for social security and medicare purposes. Besides, employees come and go.

Before actually entering an intended person on your payroll, there are a few preliminary chores to complete. For instance, if you have placed any kind of written advertisement soliciting employees, make a copy of it for your intended employee's file. Also, if the employee provided you with a written resumé, keep a copy of that, too. Also important is a written *Employment Agreement* that you and the employee sign. The agreement should provide a description of the job, hours of employment, rate of pay, pay periods, and any fringe benefits (vacations, sick pay, expense reimbursements, etc.) that you anticipate granting. Conclude the agreement with a "termination clause." This clause sets forth conditions for unilateral termination, such as tardiness, poor work product quality, alcohol, drugs, unauthorized taking of materials, tools, supplies, and so on. Give the employee a signed copy of the agreement and retain the original in that employee's file.

A payroll accounting ledger has its own brand of complexity. Aside from the name, address, SSN, marital status, W-4 certification, and gross wages of each employee, there are many columnar entries to be made. As to tax withholdings alone, as many as six separate columns may be required, depending on state and local law. We list these for you as—

1. Federal income tax (FIT)
2. Social security tax (SST)
3. Medicare tax (MDT)
4. State income tax (SIT)
5. State disability tax (SDT)
6. Local income tax (LIT)

In addition to these tax withholdings, there may be voluntary withholdings. These could be union dues, savings plans, group health payments, and loan repayments. There also could be involuntary withholdings, such as court-ordered child and/or spousal support payments, tax liens for prior deficiencies, and other judgment liens. Each of these items requires a separate columnar payroll entry of its own.

There is no universal payroll format that serves all business needs. Each business owner has to select a ledger format — or design one of his own — that best meets his particular pay and recordkeeping practices. As a summary in this regard, we present Figure 6.2. It's not just a payroll ledger that you need, you also need some system for filing the various papers on each employee. The Figure 6.2 Forms 941, 940, and W-2 are discussed below.

A variety of preprinted ledger forms and computer spreadsheets can be found in most office supply and software stores. Pick and choose among these formats. Or, engage a payroll accounting service to do the tasks for you. Whatever payrolling arrangement you make, devise your accounting periods into four separate calendar quarters for the year.

## Employer Quarterly Returns

If you have one employee and withhold so much as $1 from that employee, you become locked into a quarterly tax reporting system.

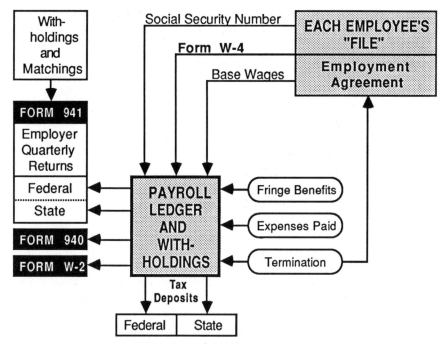

**Fig. 6.2 - Typical Records Needed on Each Employee**

In the federal domain, specifically, you are required to file Form 941: ***Employer's Quarterly Federal Tax Return.*** Similarly, states also have their version of quarterly employer returns. These are not income tax returns of the employer; they are PAYROLL tax returns. They are *in addition to* an employer's own income tax returns.

The term "quarterly" means every three months . . . without fail. These are calendar quarters, as follows:

| Quarter | Ending | Due Date |
|---------|--------|----------|
| Jan-Feb-Mar | Mar. 31 | Apr. 30 |
| Apr-May-Jun | Jun. 30 | Jul. 31 |
| Jul-Aug-Sep | Sep. 30 | Oct. 31 |
| Oct-Nov-Dec | Dec. 31 | Jan. 31 |

There are, of course, various penalties for tardiness in filing these returns. There are also penalties for tardiness in depositing the tax money with authorized Federal Tax Depository (FTD) banks. On payroll tax matters, there are penalties for every little irregularity. These penalties are intentionally designed to irritate you, and force you to cough up more employer tax money.

Each quarterly return has a 5-fold purpose. This purpose is:

1. To report total wages, tips, and other compensation paid.
2. To report total income tax withheld.
3. To compute social security tax:
   (a) employee's portion
   (b) employer's portion
4. To compute medicare tax:
   (a) employee's portion
   (b) employer's portion
5. To include backup withholding, if any.

The result of the above is a total tax and withholding for the quarter. This total is then compared with the corresponding total FTD deposits. Instructions on Form 941 tell you what to do about balances due or overpayments.

At the end of the year (due January 31), there is also employer Form 940: *Employer's Annual Federal Unemployment Tax Return*. This is an employer-only tax. Employees themselves do not contribute to the unemployment insurance fund: federal **or** state. The combined unemployment tax rate is approximately 6.2% of the first $7,000 wages paid to each employee during the year.

Also, at the end of the year there are those Forms W-2: Wage and Tax Statements to be prepared. A separate statement — consisting of some 30 entry boxes — is required for each employee. We provided you an overview of Form W-2 back in Figure 1.2.

## What If Nonemployees?

There is no question about it. Having employees is a formidable task. For self-employeds particularly, it is a drastic tax and financial imposition. It is difficult enough deriving a livelihood for oneself (and spouse). One naturally wonders: Is there some other way of getting the help needed, without the responsibility for employees?

Yes, there is another way. But you must use extreme care. You must know what you are doing. And you must do it properly.

Official guidance on "doing it properly" is sparse and unspecific. IRS **Circular E**: Employer's Tax Guide, provides some clues as to the IRS's position. In the Circular E section headed: *Who Are Employees?*, statements are made that—

*Generally, people in business for themselves are not employees. For example, doctors, lawyers, veterinarians, construction contractors, and others **in an independent trade** in which they offer their services to the public are usually not employees. . . . If you have **good reason** for treating a worker other than as an employee, you will not be liable for employment taxes on the payments to that worker. . . . To get this relief you must file all required Federal tax returns, including information returns, on a basis **consistent** with your treatment of the worker.* [Emphasis added.]

In 1987, the IRS came out with its Revenue Ruling 87-41, in which it listed 20 factors — yes, 20 — indicative of your having a "good reason" to treat workers as nonemployees. We paraphrase these 20 factors in Figure 6.3. Note that we arranged the factors into those which are indicative of employee status, and those which are indicative of nonemployee status. There is no magic number of these factors that irrefutably qualifies a worker as a nonemployee. All factors are weighed in terms of the facts and circumstances of each case.

The IRS in its Circular E concludes that—

*If you want a decision about whether a worker is an employee, file **Form SS-8**: Determination of Employee Work Status for Purposes of Federal Employment Taxes and Income Tax Withholding.*

This is a **very comprehensive** form. It consists of approximately 65 questions and 100 check-boxes. Many are trick questions designed to corner you and your worker into an irrevocable employer-employee status.

Our suggestions is: **Do not** file Form SS-8. Rarely, if ever, does the IRS rule that a worker is a nonemployee. Nevertheless, request a copy of the form but don't file it. Instead, use it for pointers in preparing a contract agreement with your worker as an independent contractor.

## FACTORS  INDICATIVE  OF  EMPLOYEE  STATUS

| | |
|---|---|
| 1. Instructions<br>- as to when, where, & how | 8. Time devoted<br>- as substantially full time |
| 2. Training<br>- under supervision of others | 9. Work on premises<br>- not permitted elsewhere |
| 3. Integration<br>- directly into daily operations | 10. Sequences set<br>- nil deviations allowed |
| 4. Personal services<br>- using own skills and talents | 11. Reports required<br>- either oral or written |
| 5. Hiring & firing<br>- subject to: by employer | 12. Paid regularly<br>- by hour, week, or month |
| 6. Continuity<br>- daily ongoing relationship | 13. Reimbursement<br>- for business & travel expense |
| 7. Hours of work<br>- when/where set & fixed | 14. Tools & materials<br>- primarily by employer |

### FACTORS  INDICATIVE  OF  NONEMPLOYEE  STATUS

15. Significant investment
  - in facilities (such as office and/or shop) and in major equipment.

16. Realization of profit or loss
  - accepting the risks of work performed in a competetive environment.

17. More than one customer
  - services for a multiple of unrelated persons or firms at the same time.

18. Available to general public
  - continuous offering of services without expectation of long-term hire.

19. "Contract" services
  - written or oral, where results are specified, not manner of performance.

20. Incurring of liability
  - if results are unsatisfactory, subject to lawsuit and rework.

**Fig. 6.3 - Factors Indicative of Employee/Nonemployee Status**

## Independent Contractors

To successfully engage nonemployees, your first task is to prepare or procure an *Independent Contractor Agreement.* With a little effort, you can do this yourself, or have your attorney or accountant prepare one for you. Use Form SS-8 and Figure 6.3 as a guide for key points you should include. Overall, the contract should spell out the self-employment type of responsibilities for the *contractor*, and your responsibilities as the *principal.*

The ultimate test as to whether a worker is a nonemployee or an employee hinges on these five points, namely:

1. Does the contractor (worker) conduct himself as a self-employed individual in a trade or business of his own?

2. Does he provide his own tools, equipment, and vehicles for the expertise portion of the contracted job or project?

3. Does he submit to the principal itemized statements and invoices (for payment) upon the completion of each job or each phase of an extended job?

4. Does he offer his services to other businesses, and is he free to do so, so long as the work agreed upon with you as principal is performed satisfactorily?

5. Does he file his own tax returns and pay his own taxes, including income taxes, social security taxes, medicare taxes, unemployment taxes, sales taxes, workmen's compensation, and other statutory liabilities imposed on other self-employeds in his geographic area?

For illustration purposes, the preamble wording to an Independent Contractor Agreement might read along the lines as follows:

*This is an Agreement between _____(called the "Principal") and_____ (called the "Contractor"). The place of business of the Principal is: _____; the place of business of the Contractor is:_____ .*

*This Agreement is entered into for the purpose of contracting for _____ services which are to be performed at one or more locations on a specific job basis. Remuneration is to be paid to the Contractor upon the satisfactory completion of each job or project, or each distinct phase thereof, and upon submission to the Principal of an itemized statement or invoice giving each job description and its applicable charges.*

Other specific contractual paragraphs should be included as appropriate. The contract should be no more than two pages in length. There should be ample room on the second page for signatures of both the Contractor and Principal, and for either a witness or a notary public.

The whole idea is that the independent contractor be a responsible person on his own. He is the type that does not need an employer to hold his hand, supervise his every move, and pay his social security, medicare, health insurance, and other employee-type benefits. If a contractor is truly independent, the IRS will have difficulty in forcing you to reclassify him as an employee.

## Impact of Reclassification

Forcefully reclassifying contractors and nonemployees as employees is a BIG SOURCE of revenue to federal and state treasuries. The revenue comes **not** from the reclassified employee. It comes from YOU as the reclassified employer. The IRS and state employment agencies take the view that you have no right to engage independent contractors, if they decide that you are doing so to avoid withholdings and to avoid paying the employer's share of social security, medicare, and unemployment taxes. They often make their reclassification decisions arbitrarily and on whim. Very few tax agents have ever been in a trade or business of their own.

If you are reclassified as an employer, vindictive tax agents can double-dip and triple-dip into your pockets. You can be forced to—

1. Pay all withholdings and payroll taxes on the reclassified employee as far back as three years.
2. Pay a 1% to 3% penalty on all gross wages you should have paid, and pay 20% to 40% penalty on the combined employer's-employee's share of social security and medicare taxes [IRC Sec. 3509].
3. Pay the income and other taxes due on the personal returns of those reclassified workers who have not filed their own returns.

The power of reclassification is sanctified in I.R. Code Section 3509: *Determination of Employer's Liability for Certain Employment Taxes*. This reclassification power has bankrupted many a small business and has left the owners destitute with personal liability . . . lasting until their deaths.

The devastation and ruthlessness of this reclassification power prompted Congress in 1978 to slap a moratorium on the IRS. In that year, Congress set forth certain "safe harbor" rules prohibiting reclassification where it was a *customary practice* in an area to engage nonemployees. The safe harbor idea was to restrain the IRS from dictating labor policies to private enterprise. In 1987, the moratorium expired. The IRS has now resumed its reclassification tactics using the 20 common law tests outlined in Figure 6.3 and described in more detail in Revenue Ruling 87-41 (1987-1 CB 296).

## Safe Harbor Rule

The safe harbor rule is founded in the Revenue Act of 1978 (section 530 thereof). The rule carves out a legislative exception to the IRS's 20-factor common law test for reclassifying a nonemployee as an employee. The thrust of the safe harbor concept is that: FOR ANY PERIOD after 1977, if a business owner has not treated a worker as an employee, such worker will be treated as an independent contractor. That is, provided that certain conditions (tests) are met.

There are three safe harbor tests. Foremost is the "reasonable basis" rationale. **Test 1** anticipates that—

The business owner has a *reasonable basis* for treating a worker as an independent contractor based on any of the following:
- (a) Judicial precedent of published rulings; or
- (b) A previous IRS audit (not necessarily for employment tax purposes) that did not result in any assessment of employment taxes for workers holding substantially similar positions; or
- (c) Long-standing recognized practice of a significant segment of the industry in which such worker was engaged.

Relying on a "reasonable basis" test is never very reliable when dealing with the IRS. With its unlimited taxpayer resources and time, the IRS gets testy and often forces an issue into Tax Court for an interpretation of key phrases. For example, the Tax Court has held that "substantially similar positions" relates to the extent of the business owner's control over the worker, rather than to the actual work performed. The Tax Court has also held that "significant segment of the industry" relates only to the business owner's immediate geographic area; it does not have to be the practice nationally (as the IRS asserts).

**Test 2** anticipates that—

> All required information returns (Forms 1099-MISC, particularly) have been filed in a manner consistent with the owner's treatment of the worker as an independent contractor, and that no W-2 forms were ever filed for such worker by the same owner.

This condition is really a matter of recordkeeping on treatment of the worker. As long as you have consistently treated him (or her) as a nonemployee, you have at least this point in your favor.

**Test 3** anticipates that—

> The business owner has not treated any worker holding a substantially similar position as an employee for employment tax purposes at any time after 1977.

This condition is rather easy to fulfill for new self-employed businesses. It is more difficult to meet for long-standing businesses. This is because sometimes a worker himself, formerly an employee, wants to become self-employed and offer his services to businesses other than your own. The IRS just doesn't seem to understand the motivational factors of self-employment as workers become more specialized and skilled.

## Toughing It Out

It is possible, though at times difficult, to run a business solely with nonemployees. It all depends on your type of business, and on your own motivations. If you are a consultant, specialist, investigator, or other professional-type entrepreneur, compensated at a high hourly rate, you could run your business entirely with nonemployees. But you have to be tough and self-disciplined to weather IRS attacks all along the way.

For example, you can engage a telephone answering service to take your phone messages and make your appointments. You can engage a secretarial service to type your letters and prepare your reports. You can engage free-lance writers, artists, technicians, handymen, and the like. You can engage — and re-engage as necessary — one or more subcontractors to do a specific job or phase of a specific project. The point is that in a "free society," you can engage and dis-engage whomever you want, provided that you strictly maintain a nonemployee posture.

There are some 80 different work occupations which have been ruled to be independent contractors (nonemployees). The rulings have been made by various Tax Courts and IRS determinations. Alphabetically, the 80 occupations span the gamut from auctioneers, buyers, loggers, tailors, to truck owner-operators. Inquire of your own tax advisor if you need more specifics.

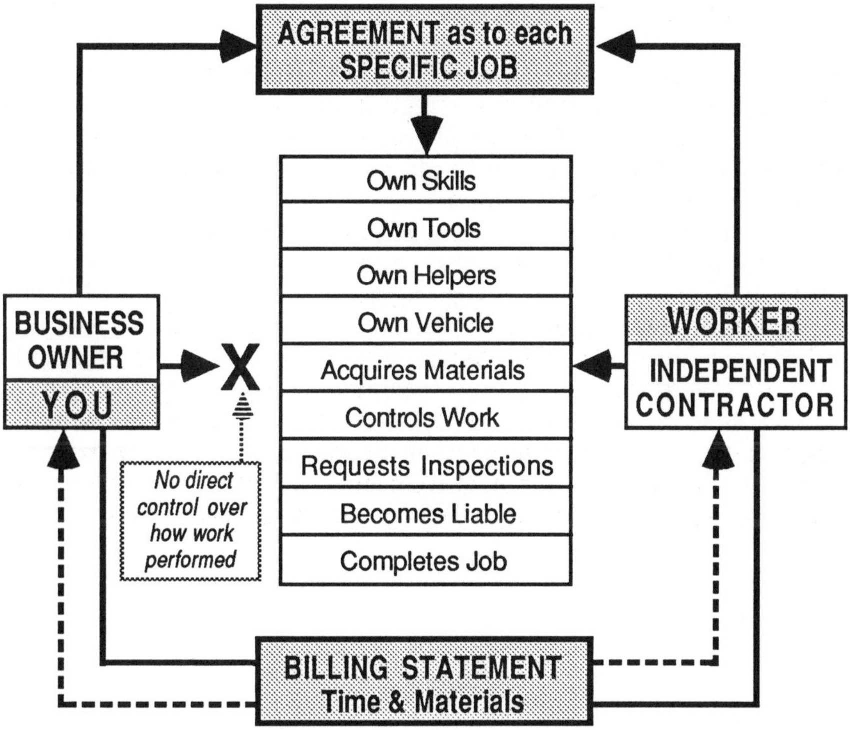

Fig. 6.4 - Toughing-It-Out Pointers on Nonemployees

Whatever you do, make sure that each worker or agency that you engage submits to you an *invoice statement* for each billing period that services are rendered. See to it that the billing periods are irregular, and that they are directly related to specific work accomplished. Simultaneous billing periods from many different independent contractors implies a recurring "payroll." The use of periodic payroll periods is generally determinative of employer-employee transactions.

Other practical tips for maintaining your nonemployees are presented in Figure 6.4. We have presented only the most significant features required. If you position yourself squarely on the indicated points, at least you have a fighting chance of winning your case against reclassification.

There is nothing improper about engaging employees and nonemployees in the same business. The fact that you may have one common law employee, in and of itself, does not mandate that all of your workers have to be employees. But you do have to draw and maintain a clear line of distinction between the two classes of workers. Treat each class (employees/nonemployees) as a separate body of workers. Within each class, make sure that the functions performed are workwise similar.

Do not cross over the two classes — by making employees nonemployees, or nonemployees employees — just because you think you can save money by doing so. Any crossover made upon your initiative is guaranteed to be used against you for classifying **all** of your workers as employees. For any crossover to be upheld in your favor, the action must be initiated solely by the worker himself/herself. It must be made voluntarily by the worker, without encouragement or discouragement on your part. If this is truly the case, be sure to document chronologically all of the facts and circumstances of the worker's request for nonemployee status.

# 7

# DEPRECIATION, ETC.

For Proper Depreciation Accounting, Form 4562 Is Your MUST. It And Its Worksheet Accommodate Listed Property, Sec. 179 Property, MACRS Property, Pre-MACRS Property, Improvements, Amortized Costs And Other Capital Items Used In A Trade Or Business. Every Passenger Auto (Luxury Or Otherwise) Is Subject To Stringent Depreciation Rules Under Sec. 280F. Nonpersonal Use Items Benefit From Accelerated Cost Recovery Under Sec. 168 Class Lives. Amortized Costs Are Generally Straight-Line Recovered Over 60 Months. When Assets No Longer Serve A Business Need, Full "Dispositional Accounting" (Via Form 4797) Is Required.

As you probably already know, depreciation is a deduction allowance for the exhaustion, wear, tear, and obsolescence of certain capital assets used in a trade or business. The statutory recognition of this allowance is Section 167(a): Depreciation: General Rule.

Although the concept of depreciation allowance has been around for years (at least since 1954), it has been much maligned by the IRS. The malignity arises because of the phrase: *reasonable allowance for* . . . contained in Section 167(a). Whenever a tax law uses the word "reasonable," it is a sure bet that the IRS will challenge whatever interpretation you make of the word. For an agency with so much power, reasonableness is not the IRS's forte.

In 1981, smarting from industry complaints against the IRS, Congress changed the concept of depreciation to one of **cost recovery**. It enacted Section 168: Accelerated Cost Recovery System. Simultaneously, it amended Section 179 to read: Election to Expense Certain Depreciable Business Assets. Section 179 was an effort to grant some relief to small business owners against the anticipated harshness of the IRS's interpretation of Section 168. Section 168, by the way, has been amended numerous times since 1981, the latest amendment being 1990. The many amendments are testimony to the insistence of the IRS in disregarding the intent of Congress.

Section 168 (as amended in 1990) consists of approximately 8,000 words. Obviously, all we intend to address in this chapter are those provisions which most directly affect small business owners. As a guide in this respect, we will focus primarily on Form 4562: Depreciation and Amortization. As an IRS-generated form, the 4562 dissects the concept of depreciation cost recovery and treats it in many different ways. This is why we included the "Etc." in the chapter heading above.

## Introduction to Form 4562

Whether you run your business as a sole proprietorship or a a partnership, there is one tax form you must use. This is Form 4562: *Depreciation and Amortization*. Below this title is a subtitle which reads: Including Information on Listed Property. ("Listed property" is that which has personal and business use mixed.) Next, a small headnote instruction reads—

*See separate instructions.*
*Attach this form to your return.*

Then, following your name and TID (either EIN or SSN), there is a full-width blank line identified as—

*Business or activity to which this form relates:*

It is doubtful that you can operate any trade or business, self-employed or otherwise, without ever having to use Form 4562. For example, take the everyday likelihood of using one's personal auto for business purposes. If you want to claim so much as $1 of auto expenses in a proprietorship, an entry item on Schedule C (Form 1040) says—

*Car and truck expenses*
*(attach Form 4562)*

Whether you claim depreciation on the car or not, if you want an expense deduction for it, you have to use Form 4562. We'll get to the reason for this later.

In the meantime, we should introduce you to Form 4562, even if you are already aware of it. Other than pure depreciation, it contains a lot of items which are offshoots from the depreciation and listed property rules. Accordingly, we present in Figure 7.1 a highly abridged format of Form 4562. As you can see, we are stressing its **functional** content, rather than specific line numbers and words. The official form contains about 50 line entries, 25 lines of which have 6 columns or more. If you don't have an official Form 4562 in your possession, you should get one before too long.

There is really only one message for you in Figure 7.1. It is that there are numerous variants of the depreciation concept. This means that however you may have deducted depreciation in the past, you have to change your thinking processes. Claiming depreciation on passenger vehicles today is truly a nightmare. Vehicle depreciation is severely limited by mixed-use and luxury-use rules.

We are using Figure 7.1 primarily as an outline as we proceed through this chapter. In doing so, we will try to keep things as condensed as possible. We will avoid those matters which are unlikely to be of interest to self-employed owners of small businesses.

## The $10,000 Election

There is one item on Form 4562 which is intended strictly for small businesses. This is Part I in Figure 7.1 identified as: *Election to Expense Certain Tangible Property*. This is a $10,000 election. It applies to tangible property actively used in a trade or business. By "actively used," we mean being used in business at least more than 50% of the time (as contrasted to any personal use). Up to $10,000 can be expensed currently rather than being capitalized and depreciated over a prescribed period of use.

The election to expense (rather than depreciate) is prescribed by subsections (a) and (b) of Section 179: *Election to Expense*

| Form 4562 | DEPRECIATION AND AMORTIZATION | Tax Year |
|---|---|---|

**Part I** — Election to Expense Certain Tangible Property

- ■ $10,000 limit
- ■ Taxable Income limit
- ■ Total elected cost
- ■ Carryover of unused

Note: If you have "Listed Property", Complete Part V

**Part II** — MACRS Depreciation: Current Year

- ☐ 8 property classes
- ☐ Business use basics
- ☐ 7 columnar entries
- ☐ Method/convention

Do Not Include Listed Property

**Part III** — Other Depreciation: Prior Years(s)

- ■ From Worksheet 4562W
- ■ Pre MACRS
- ■ Prior MACRS
- ■ Improvements

Do Not Include Listed Property

**Part IV** — Summary: Enter on "Appropriate Lines" of Return

- ☐ Listed property (p.2)
- ☐ Nonpersonal items

**Part V** — Listed Property - Autos, Phones, Computers, etc.

Section A: Depreciation Deduction
- ■ 9 columnar entries
- ■ Over 50% BUP

Section B: Information Regarding Use of Vehicles
- ☐ 4 mileage questions   ☐ 3 other questions   ☐ 6 vehicles

Section C: Questions for Employers
- ■ 5 questions   ■ Company cars   ■ Employee personal uses

**Part VI** — Amortization (of Capitalized Expenditures)

- ☐ Current Amortization
- ☐ Prior Amortization
- ☐ 6 columnar entries
- ☐ Specific code sections

Enter on "Other Expenses/Deductions" Line

**Fig. 7.1 - Abridged Format/Contents of Form 4562**

*Certain Depreciable Business Assets.* The phrase "certain business assets" excludes land, workplace buildings, intangible assets (such as goodwill), and fixed improvements to real estate. The election is intended to apply to the use of tools, instruments, machinery, equipment, work stations, storage cabinets, and nonpersonal-use vehicles. Although passenger vehicles can qualify for the election, the limitation rules are so stringent that the effort is not worth it. For automobiles, the election is limited to $2,660 x the business-use fraction (only if this fraction is greater than 50%).

The $10,000 expense election applies *each year* that qualified assets are purchased and placed in service. Property is not "purchased" if it is acquired from a related party, decedent, exchange, or other transaction requiring the use of a carryover basis. It is "placed in service" the first moment it is used *productively* in a trade or business. Thus, if one buys and uses a $10,000 piece of equipment in December, he can expense the entire amount at one time. This is so, even if the equipment otherwise would be required to be depreciated over five years.

If one buys and uses more than $10,000 of qualifying assets, but less than $200,000, the excess over $10,000 can be depreciated under the regular class-life rules. However, if one's taxable income (net profit) from the business is less than $10,000 (computed without the election), the expensed amount is limited to the taxable income. The unused portion of the $10,000 can be carried over to the following year or years.

Part I of Form 4562 is quite self-explanatory, if you follow the line-by-line instructions thereon. This is why, for this particular chapter, we encourage you to have an official form at your side as you read along. You do not have to exercise the $10,000 election option, but once you do, it becomes irrevocable.

## MACRS Depreciation Explained

The main thrust of Form 4562 is its Part II (in Figure 7.1): MACRS Depreciation. The acronym MACRS stands for: Modified Accelerated Cost Recovery System. In 1981, the ACRS system was instituted. It featured accelerated depreciation across the board for all business use of recoverable assets. It shortened the cost recovery periods substantially. The ACRS system was "modified" in 1986 and again in 1988, by "switching" from accelerated to straight line depreciation about half-way through each recovery period. Simultaneously MACRS extended the ACRS recovery periods.

To illustrate the recovery-period modifications, take autos and computers, for example. These are everyday capital assets used in any trade or business, large or small. Under ACRS, the statutory cost recovery period for autos and computers was three years. Under MACRS, the cost recovery is five years for the same assets.

Under MACRS, all depreciable assets are assigned the following property classes and recovery periods [Sec. 168(c) and (e)]:

(1)    3-year property;
(2)    5-year property;
(3)    7-year property;
(4)    10-year property;
(5)    15-year property;
(6)    20-year property;
(7)    residential rentals (27.5 yrs); or
(8)    nonresidential realty (31.5 yrs)

These eight classes of depreciable property are displayed quite prominently on Form 4562. You can't miss them in its Part II.

To give you some idea of the kinds of depreciable items that fall into classes (1) through (6), we present Figure 7.2. Although we list all six classes, we doubt that a self-employed business owner would have much need for classes (5) and (6).

There are three depreciation methods allowed under MACRS. These are:

(a)    200% declining balance, switching to straight line for classes (1) through (4);
(b)    150% declining balance, switching to straight line for classes (3) through (6); and
(c)    straight line depreciation for classes (7) and (8), or *elective* straight line for classes (1) through (6) [Sec. 168(b)(5)].

The IRS has prepared MACRS depreciation tables for all the property classes above. These tables list the percentages to be applied each year that the property is used in business. The allowable depreciation deduction is determined by multiplying the unadjusted or original basis of the capital asset by the listed percentage for the appropriate year in the recovery period.

| RECOVERY CLASS | | CLASS LIFESPAN | EXAMPLES |
|---|---|---|---|
| (1) | 3 year | 4 yrs or less | Power tools, dies, jigs, R&D items, computer software, carts & trays |
| (2) | 5 year | 4 to 10 yrs | Autos, light trucks, computers; equipment: office, shop, medical |
| (3) | 7 year | 10 to 16 yrs | Furniture, fixtures , & furnishings; heavy duty trucks, machinery, equip. |
| (4) | 10 year | 16 to 20 yrs | Boats, airplanes, hangars, storage sheds, barns, horticultural structures |
| (5) | 15 year | 20 to 25 yrs | Water, power, & communication systems; fruit bearing trees & vines |
| (6) | 20 year | 25 yrs or more | Municipal sewers, recycling plants, warehouses, bridges |

**Fig. 7.2 - Classification of Property for Cost Recovery Purposes**

Entry of the depreciation amount on Form 4562 (Part II) is limited to the year of placement in service only. This creates a problem of keeping track of the depreciation on prior-year assets, and of the cumulative depreciation year after year. This is where the IRS's Depreciation Worksheet comes in handy.

## The Depreciation Worksheet

Part III of Form 4562 accommodates all other depreciation deductions not permissible in Part II. Part III includes all depreciation computations under all prior rules, for those assets placed in service prior to the current taxable year. For this, the IRS has prepared a very useful worksheet, titled: *Depreciation Worksheet.* As of this moment, the IRS has not assigned it an official form number. We, therefore, call it: Form 4562W (the "W", of course, meaning "worksheet"). On the back of this worksheet there are those MACRS percentage tables mentioned above. Having these percentages readily available is a real convenience.

For your instructional benefit, we present in Figure 7.3 a listing of the columnar entries that appear on Form 4562W. Be aware that we have rearranged the columnar entries vertically, instead of horizontally as they appear on the official worksheet. The vertical arrangement is more conducive to instructional explanations. At this point, we want to call your attention first to Columns 5 and 7.

| Col. | Heading | Prop. A | Prop. B | Prop. C |
|------|---------|---------|---------|---------|
| **Depreciation Worksheet: Backup to Form 4562** | | | | |
| 1. | Description of Property | | | |
| 2. | Date Placed in Service | | | |
| 3. | Cost or Other Basis | | | |
| 4. | Business Use % | | | |
| 5. | Section 179 Deduction | | | |
| 6. | Depreciation Prior Years | | | |
| 7. | Basis for Depreciation | | | |
| 8. | Method/Convention | | | |
| 9. | Recovery Period | | | |
| 10. | Rate or Table % | | | |
| 11. | Depreciation Deduction | | | |

*Note:* On the official form, the headings are horizontal, not vertical as shown above. The worksheet accommodates up to 36 horizontal entry lines. Continuation sheets may be used as needed. We suggest showing TOTALS for Columns 3, 5, 6, and 11.

**Fig. 7.3 - Columnar Headings on Depreciation Worksheet**

Note that Column 5 in Figure 7.3 is headed: Section 179 Deduction. This is that $10,000 election option we told you about earlier. To explain the use of this column, let's take two examples: a $9,000 asset and a $15,000 asset, each placed in service in different years. Assume that the expense election for each of the two years was properly taken.

As to the $9,000 asset, once Section 179 is elected, there is no remaining depreciation. Therefore, the $9,000 is entered in Column 5 and zero is entered in Column 7. As to the $15,000 asset,

$10,000 is entered in Column 5; $5,000 is entered in Column 7; and $1,000 is entered in Column 11 (using the MACRS percentage tables: 20% x $5,000). The point that we are making is that you have to keep a running record of all Section 179 elections ever made. You do this until each Section 179 asset is properly removed from service. There is no provision for doing this on Form 4562; this is where the worksheet comes in handy.

Especially note that Column 8 in Figure 7.3 is headed: Method/Convention. There are three MACRS depreciation methods (listed above) and three MACRS conventions. A "convention" is an averaging rule when property is placed in service or taken out of service. Instead of showing actual dates in Column 8, you can use (Mid-month (MM), (b) Mid-quarter (MQ), or (c) Half-year (HY). The mid-month convention is required for all realty assets; the mid-quarter convention is required when more than 40% of Class (1) through (6) assets are placed in service during the last three months of the year. The half-year conventions can be used for all other depreciable assets whether placed in, or taken out of, service during the early part of the year or later in the year.

### "Listed Property" Explained

If you'll glance back at Figure 7.1 again, you'll note that in Parts II and III, there is a bold-lettered instruction. It reads—

*Do Not Include Listed Property*

In Part I, there is an italicized instruction which reads—

*Note: If you have any "Listed Property," complete Part V*

So, "What is 'listed property'?" you ask.

Listed property is mixed business- and personal-use property. It is a type that is a "natural" for personal use under the guise of a business purpose. Statutorily, it is defined as—

(i) *any passenger automobile* [Sec. 280F(d)(4)(A)],
(ii) *any other property used as a means of transportation* [boats, airplanes, campers],
(iii) *any property of a type generally used for entertainment, recreation, or amusement,*
(iv) *any computer or peripheral equipment,*

*(v)    any cellular telephone (or other similar telecommunications
equipment), and*

*(vi)   any other property of a type specified by the* [IRS] *by
regulation.* [Emphasis added.]

The idea behind designating the above items as listed property is
to force you to keep adequate records on the business use of that
property. You must keep records on number of times used, number
of hours used, or number of miles used (whichever is appropriate).
No convincing records: no depreciation deduction. It's that simple.
The purpose of keeping records is to establish a *business-use
percentage* at the end of each year. Once you have this percentage,
you can then use Section A of Part V (in Figure 7.1) to compute
your depreciation allowance.

Part V consists of three subparts, namely:

Section A  —  Depreciation Deduction
Section B  —  Information Regarding Use of Vehicles
Section C  —  Questions for Employers Who Provide Vehicles
                 for Use by Their Employees

As to Section C, if you are an employer who furnishes a "company
car" to one or more employees, you should get the official
instruction to Form 4562 and read up on the rules thereto. The rules
focus on certain written policy statements prohibiting personal use
of company vehicles. These rules alone will make you try harder to
engage nonemployees rather than employees. Nonemployees will
provide their own vehicles for business purposes.

Before starting on Part V, you need in hand the acquisition
document (purchase invoice) on each item that you intend to list.
You'll need it for description, date, and cost basis purposes.

Section A of Part V has columnar entries very similar to those on
the depreciation worksheet in Figure 7.3. The entry in Column 4:
Business Use %, is the target for scrutiny by the IRS. This
percentage times the Cost or Other Basis (Column 3), establishes the
Business Basis for Depreciation (Column 7). The worksheet,
however, CANNOT BE USED FOR LISTED PROPERTY. Such
property must be entered in Section A year after year. This requires
hand-entered notations directly on Form 4562 for keeping track of
the prior depreciation taken, for each listed property item.

## Business Mileage Log

Any automobile or passenger-carrying truck or van is automatically classified as listed property (see above). This means that great effort must be expended to establish the business-use percentage of such vehicle(s). The kind of effort required is signified by the following headnote questions in Section A, Part V, of Form 4562:

a. *Do you have evidence to support the business use claimed?* ☐ *Yes* ☐ *No.*

b. *If "Yes," is the evidence written?* ☐ *Yes* ☐ *No.*

With respect to any passenger-carrying vehicle, the only acceptable written evidence is a **business mileage log.** Such log should be "regularly posted." This means no less frequently than once a week. Preferably, the posting should be done upon the completion of each business trip, citing the destination, purpose, and miles. We know this sounds tedious and boring, but once you get into the habit of making entries into your log, it is not all that bad. You need to do this for *each separate vehicle* used in your trade or business. A timely prepared mileage log will truly work wonders when your car and truck expenses are IRS challenged.

In the front of each log, enter your odometer reading at the beginning and ending of each year. You will need the grand total miles driven (business *and* nonbusiness) — from January 1 through December 31 — for computing your business-use percentage. You will also need to reconstruct your total commuting miles for the year, if any. Commuting is going from your place of residence to place of work, and returning home. Commuting is treated as nonbusiness use, unless you can establish extraordinary business reasons to the contrary.

With a good auto/truck mileage log, you are in a sound position to complete Section B, Part V, on Form 4562. This section — Information Regarding Use of Vehicles — requires specific mileage data for each vehicle (auto, truck, van) used for business during the year. You also have to indicate whether you use it, a partner uses it, an investor uses it, or a family member or friend uses it. In Figure 7.4, we indicate the kind of information that you must enter on the

| Section B, Part V (LISTED PROPERTY), Form 4562 | | | |
|---|---|---|---|
| **During the year -** | Vehicle 1 | Vehicle 2 | Vehicle 3 |
| 1 Total business miles | | | |
| 2 Total commuting miles | $BUP = \dfrac{Item\ 1}{Item\ 4} = \%$ | | |
| 3 Total other personal miles | | | |
| 4 Grand total miles driven | | | |

| **How Vehicle Used -** | Yes | No | Yes | No | Yes | No |
|---|---|---|---|---|---|---|
| 5 Was it available for personal use during off duty hours? | | | | | | |
| 6 Was it used primarily by a more than 5% owner or related person? | | | | | | |
| 7 Is another vehicle available for personal use? | | | | | | |

Fig. 7.4 - Required Mileage Information on Passenger Vehicles

official form. We also indicate the computation of your business-use percentage (BUP).

You must complete the Figure 7.4 informational entries regardless of what method you use for claiming your auto/truck expenses. Actually, there are three such methods, namely:

(a) Standard mileage rate (about 28¢/mi) for the business mileage only;
(b) Depreciation plus operating expenses, times the business-use percentage;
(c) Lease payments plus operating expenses, times the business-use percentage.

For each vehicle, you may use one-only of these methods: **not** portions of each. However, you may use method (a) for vehicle 1; method (b) for vehicle 2; and method (c) for vehicle 3.

## Luxury Auto Limits

In October 1987, the IRS defined a "luxury auto" as any passenger vehicle costing more than $12,060 (including sales tax and accessories). Can you believe this! The luxury threshold amount is adjusted upward each year (in $100 increments) for auto price inflation.

In 1992, the luxury threshold became $12,660. For placing a vehicle in service that year, the maximum 5-year MACRS depreciation would be $12,660. This is the depreciation limit, no matter what the initial vehicle cost might be.

Where does the IRS get this notion of a luxury auto value?

Answer: From Section 280F of the IR Code. This section is titled: *Limitation on Depreciation for Luxury Automobiles*.

Subsection 280F(a) goes on to spell out the yearly depreciation limits (starting in 1990) as follows:

   *(i)    $2,560 for the 1st taxable year in the recovery period,*
   *(ii)   $4,100 for the 2nd taxable year in the recovery period,*
   *(iii)  $2,450 for the 3rd taxable year in the recovery period, and*
   *(iv)   $1,475 for each succeeding year in the recovery period.*

These yearly depreciation (cost recovery) limits are based on 100% business use. The IRS absolutely refuses to accept 100% business use of a passenger-carrying vehicle. Its argument is that you surely must have driven your spouse, child, or friend to a shopping center at some time, or several times. The maximum business-use percentage the IRS will accept is 95%. This acceptance is only if you can produce an outstanding mileage log record, and can show that you have one or more purely personal-use vehicles. Otherwise, each year's depreciation limits above have to be factored by your business-use percentages [Sec. 280F(a)(2)].

If your business-use percentage drops to 50% or below, certain *recapture*-of-depreciation rules apply [Sec. 280F(b)(2)(A)]. In essence, the recapture amount is the excess of MACRS depreciation over straight-line depreciation. This excess, if any, is treated as *other income* on the business portion of your tax return. With auto price inflation adjustments to the MACRS tables [Sec. 280F(d)(7)], this "other income" becomes another tax accounting annoyance. All of this operating recapture is irrelevant, however, if your bona fide business use is more than 50%.

After the fifth year, if you are still using a vehicle that initially cost you more than the luxury threshold, your yearly depreciation thereafter is limited to $1,475 (plus an inflation adjustment).

For example, suppose you paid $29,660 for an auto in 1992. (Assume, for simplicity, 100% business use.) After five years you have taken the maximum depreciation recovery of $12,660. This leaves $17,000 of initial cost unrecovered. But you still continue to use the auto. How much depreciation can you take?

For a vehicle initially placed in service in 1992, you can take $1,575 for each year past the fifth that you continue to use the vehicle. At this rate, it will take you about 10 years more ($17,000 ÷ $1,575/yr) to recover your full initial cost. That's 15 years in all.

The IRS message, of course, is: Don't buy a luxury auto for business purposes.

## Luxury Auto Leasing

If the nature of your self-employed business is such that a luxury auto is a "must," you have an attractive option. You can lease the car instead of buying it. That is, provided you get a pure lease rather than a lease with option to buy. A pure lease is when you can turn the car in at the end of the contract . . . and walk away.

If you lease an auto for business, whether luxury or otherwise, you still have to establish your business-use percentage (BUP). There's no way around it. This means that you still have to keep a contemporaneous mileage log, with its collateral supporting evidence.

If you do have a pure lease, there is considerable simplicity in your tax accounting. You have only to keep track of your operating expenses (gas, oil, repairs, insurance, etc.) and your lease payments. Furthermore, if you had month-to-month leases, and used two or three different cars for the year, you don't have to distinguish between them. You can combine all the operating expenses and all the lease payments. You can even combine the business miles, so long as you keep track of the grand total business-plus-nonbusiness miles driven. That BUP again.

When leasing, your tax computation is as simple as 1, 2, 3. The procedure is as follows:

1. Total operating expenses       _____
2. Total lease payments           _____
3. ADD items 1 and 2              _____
4. MULTIPLY item 3 by your BUP    _____

Is there a tax catch to all of this leasing?

Yes; of course there is.  As a taxpayer-lessee, you are subject to inclusion of phantom income.  That is, you have to **include in your gross income** a specified amount (as determined by the IRS) each year, corresponding to the initial fair market value (FMV) of the leased vehicle [Sec. 280F(c)(2), (3)].

The IRS has prepared a number of Leased Auto Dollar (Inclusion) Tables.  Different tables are used, depending on the calendar year in which the lease term begins.  The tables extend from approximately $12,800 in vehicle value to as high as $250,000 in value.  Selected portions of the "Inclusion Table" for 1990 are presented in Figure 7.5.  The indicated amounts give you an idea of the dollar magnitude of the "phantom income" that you have to show on your return.

## Leased Business Auto Table

### Income Inclusion Amount for Autos Leased in 1990

| FMV (Fair Market Value) | Tax Year During Lease | | | | |
| --- | --- | --- | --- | --- | --- |
| | 1st (1990) | 2nd (1991) | 3rd (1992) | 4th (1993) | 5th (1994) |
| $ 12,800 * | $ 0 | $ 0 | $ 0 | $ 1 | $ 2 |
| 20,000 | 97 | 214 | 317 | 382 | 445 |
| 30,000 | 239 | 526 | 778 | 936 | 1,084 |
| 35,000 | 309 | 677 | 1,004 | 1,206 | 1,396 |
| 40,000 | 378 | 829 | 1,230 | 1,476 | 1,707 |
| 50,000 | 517 | 1,133 | 1,680 | 2,016 | 2,331 |
| 60,000 ▲ | 663 | 1,452 | 2,153 | 2,584 | 2,985 |

\* This is the maximum cost recovery for a buyer-owned vehicle over a 5-yr period (100% BUP).

▲ The official table lists 90 separate FMV values

Caution: These selections are for illustration purposes only. Obtain official table for your lease year.

Fig. 7.5 - Selections from IRS Leased Auto Inclusion Table

Instructions in Regulation 1.280F-7T(a) direct that the inclusion amount be determined as follows:

1. Corresponding to the FMV, select from the applicable table (and lease term year) the dollar amount prescribed.
2. Prorate the dollar amount for the number of days in the lease term in the taxable year at issue.
3. Multiply the prorated dollar amount by the BUP for that year.
4. Include the computed amount (for the year at issue) on your tax return at the line marked: **Other income**. Identify as "Sec. 280F(c)(3)."

The only relief from the inclusion requirement is when an auto is rented for less than 30 days. This exception [Sec. 280F(c)(2)] is to accommodate away-from-home business trips where occasional car rentals are used.

## The Summary on Form 4562

Part IV of the official form carries the one-word heading: *Summary*. It is a depreciation-only summary. It does not include operating expenses of any kind. Said expenses go elsewhere on your return. The Form 4562 summary is limited strictly to the depreciation (including the Section 179 election) shown in Parts I, II, III, and V (Listed Property).

Because the instructions to Parts I, II, and III forbid the inclusion of listed properties, the very first summary item in Part IV is:

*Listed property — Enter amount from* [page 2].

As mentioned previously, once you enter a listed property item in Section A of Part V, it stays there year after year. This includes luxury autos, whether bought or leased. No depreciation is allowed on a leased vehicle, but you still have to show all other information requested (as in Figure 7.4). All listed property stays on Form 4562 until it is either sold, traded in, converted (to personal use), lease expired, abandoned, or junked. When any of these events takes place, there are other tax accounting rules that come into play.

For space reasons on the official form, all other depreciation amounts are grand totaled together for a single entry on one line. This single-line entry includes—

Part I    — The Section 179 election
Part II   — Current year MACRS depreciation
Part III  — Prior year MACRS and other depreciation

The "other depreciation" includes all pre-MACRS depreciation allowances EXCEPT business use of home. The business use of one's home is indeed listed property. However, a special form (discussed in Chapter 4) applies. Office-at-home depreciation is a special matter which we'll get to in a moment.

In the Part IV Summary, there is one grant total boxed space for all Form 4562 depreciation. The instruction at the total box says—

*Enter here and on the appropriate lines of your return.*

This generalized wording is used because Form 4562 is attachable to any type of tax return: proprietorship, partnership, corporation, trust, or other. The "appropriate line" on any of these returns is that line which clearly reads: **Depreciation.**

For example, on Schedule C (Form 1040) for a sole proprietorship, there is an expense line which reads (in part):

*Depreciation (see instructions).*

Similarly, on Form 1065 for a partnership, there is a deduction line which reads:

*Depreciation (see instructions).*

In both of these cases, the instructions tell you— [LESS that]

*amount of depreciation reported elsewhere on your return.*

This kind of instruction leaves matters open for any special depreciation forms, such as Form 8829 (Business Use of Home).

Once your summary depreciation from Form 4562 is entered on your return, it combines with other expenses and deductions for determining the net profit or loss for your business.

## Depreciation of Home

Your home is a piece of real estate, provided it is built on, or set on, a parcel of land. As such, you are entitled to a depreciation allowance for the business-use portion of the building structure. Depreciation is allowed, however, only if you own — or are buying — the home. If you are renting your home, you can take the business-use portion of the rent paid, similar to that of leasing a vehicle.

Real estate is MACRS classed as 27.5-year (residential) and 31.5-year (nonresidential) property. Any business use of your home constitutes a "cross" between these two MACRS classes. For simplicity, we use 30 years. All real estate is depreciated straight line; no acceleration of any kind is permitted. Thus, 30 years straight line converts into a 3.33% rate of depreciation each year (100% ÷ 30 yrs).

The big issue with real estate is that the land on which your residence sits does **not** depreciate. This means that the very first thing you have to do is establish the *land fraction* of your home site. For this, you need the latest assessed valuation of your property by the County Assessor. Most Assessors (for property tax purposes) notify home owners each year of the assessed valuations in the following form:

| | | |
|---|---|---|
| Land | $_____ | |
| Improvements | $_____ | (buildings) |
| Total | $_____ | |

The land fraction of your property is simply the dollar assessment of your land divided by the total dollar assessment of land plus building. This land fraction — be it 20%, 40%, or whatever — is treated as the "official fraction" by the IRS. That is, provided the local assessors follow uniform practices statewide. Assessed values are for property tax purposes only; they may have no relationship whatever to fair market values. Always keep this point in mind.

Your next step is to determine whichever of the following is **the smaller,** namely:

(a) your home's adjusted cost (or other) basis, or
(b) your home's fair market value.

Your adjusted cost basis is your purchase cost (or other acquisition basis) *plus* fixed improvements up to the date that you start using the home for business purposes. The fair market value is the latest valuation of your property by a professional real estate appraiser. If you've owned your home more than five years, your adjusted cost basis is probably lower than the fair market value.

With the above information, you proceed to compute your allowable business-use depreciation as follows:

**Step 1.** Enter adjusted cost basis or fair market value, whichever is LOWER    $_____

**Step 2.** Enter value of land. (Assessor's land fraction x Step 1.)    _____

**Step 3.** Basis of building. *Subtract* Step 2 from Step 1.    _____

**Step 4.** Business basis of building. *Multiply* Step 3 by percentage in Part I, Form 8829    _____

**Step 5.** Enter depreciation percentage (for 30 years straight line depreciation)    3.33%

**Step 6.** *Depreciation allowable. Multiply* Step 4 by Step 5. Then follow instructions on Form 8829, Part III    $_____

Form 8829 (Business Use of Home) has no provision for keeping track of the cumulative prior-year depreciation allowances on your home. For this purpose, we recommend using the Depreciation Worksheet (Form 4562W) described above. Make a distinctive separate entry on this worksheet. You do not want to inadvertently add your home depreciation to the depreciation summary on Form 4562.

## Improvements vs. Repairs

There is a perpetual struggle between the IRS and small business owners over the issue of improvements versus repairs. If you so much as add a nut and bolt to a piece of depreciable equipment, or replace a part thereto, the IRS wants to depreciate said expenditures over the entire class life of the property item. This whole affair is a paranoidal stance with the IRS. By forcing you to reclassify repair-type items as improvement-type items, the IRS can increase your tax markedly.

It is pretty well recognized that substantial improvements to property already in service are capital expenditures. They are depreciated over time, and not currently expensed as repairs. The statutory groundwork for this is set forth in IRC Section 263(a): Capital Expenditure, to wit:

*No* [current] *deduction shall be allowed for—*
*(1)  Any amount paid . . . for permanent improvements or betterments made to increase the value of any property or estate.*
*(2)  Any amount paid in restoring property or in making good the exhaustion thereof for which an allowance* [for depreciation] *is or has been made.*

There is a serious flaw in this tax law. It is the phrase: "any amount." This gets us into the $1 and $2 arguments with overzealous IRS persons. In all due fairness, the IRS uses a $100 rule of thumb. If the expenditure on a depreciable asset is $100 or more, the IRS's gut reaction is to classify that expenditure as an improvement. A $100 expenditure on a $1,000 asset may be significant (at 10%), but the same expenditure on a $10,000 asset may be insignificant (at 1%). Ordinary common sense tells you that an improvement—

(1)  adds to the value of the property; or
(2)  substantially prolongs its useful life; or
(3)  adapts it to a new and different use.

Regulation 1.263(a)-1(b) states very clearly that—

*Amounts paid or incurred for **incidental repairs and maintenance** of property are not capital expenditures.* [Emphasis added.]

What are often "incidental repairs and maintenance" to a business owner generally are improvements to the IRS. Interpretation objectivity is not an IRS forte. Maximum revenue is.

Common sense suggests that if an expenditure is *de minimis or insubstantial* relative to the initial cost basis of the asset itself, it should be treated automatically as a repair. Just what is de minimis or insubstantial has never been defined in Section 263. However, Section 280A(g): Special Rule for Certain Rental Use, defines its de minimis exception as 14/365 or 3.83%. The IRS tries to avoid committing itself to any exception to capitalizing restoration-type expenditures.

Our suggestion is to use a de minimis threshold of 5%. Should your expenditures to an in-service asset exceed 5% of its initial cost, you are probably wise to depreciate said amount. Do so on your Depreciation Worksheet immediately below the property item to which the "improvement" relates.

## Amortizing Intangibles

The very last item on Form 4562 Part VI, titled: *Amortization*. Here is where you enter the cumulation of all expenditures that you incurred for so-called *intangible assets*. Ordinarily, these are costs which you incur over a period of time, to better position your business for competitive and regulatory reasons. They are "intangible" in the sense that they do not represent the lump-sum purchase price of an item of property that is depreciable elsewhere on Form 4562. The cumulative expenditures become "assets" in the sense that they are prescribed by the tax code as being *capitalized* rather than being expensed currently.

The amortization concept is another of those refinements of the IRS's intransigence towards business operations. Stretching out otherwise legitimate expenditures always maximizes revenue.

The following is a list of the types of expenditures that are classed as amortizable (capital) assets in the IR Code:

| | | | |
|---|---|---|---|
| (1) | Pollution control facilities | — | Sec. 169 |
| (2) | Certain bond premiums | — | Sec. 171 |
| (3) | Publisher's circulation expenditures | — | Sec. 173 |
| (4) | Research and experimental costs | — | Sec. 174 |
| (5) | Cost of Acquiring a Lease | — | Sec. 178 |
| (6) | Expenditures for fertilizers, lime, etc. | — | Sec. 180 |
| (7) | Reforestation expenditures | — | Sec. 194 |
| (8) | Business startup costs | — | Sec. 195 |
| (9) | Corporate organization costs | — | Sec. 248 |
| (10) | Intangible drilling costs | — | Sec. 263 |
| (11) | Preproduction expenses | — | Sec. 263A |
| (12) | Mine development costs | — | Sec. 616 |
| (13) | Partnership formation fee | — | Sec. 709 |

Most of the above costs are amortizable over 60 months (five years), using the mid-month convention. The allowable cost recovery is pure straight line: no accelerations. However, in some cases you may elect to amortize certain expenditures over three years, or you can elect to stretch them out to 10 years [Sec. 59(e)].

Whatever amortization period you use, you must state in Part VI of Form 4562 the specific Code section on which you are relying. Where cost recovery began in a prior year, there should be one or more *amortization schedules* on your Depreciation Worksheet.

The amortization summary in Part VI consists of just three lines, namely:

Line 1. Amortization of costs that begin during current year. _____

Line 2. Amortization of costs that began before current year. _____

Line 3. Total [of lines 1 and 2]. Enter here and on "Other expenses" or "Other deductions" lines of your tax return. _____

There is a point being made by the line 3 instruction. It is that the word "Amortization" does **not** appear on any of the preprinted lines on your tax forms. Therefore, you intentionally have to write in the word on the other expenses/deductions lines of your business returns.

## Disposition of Assets

Once you enter an item on Form 4562: Depreciation and Amortization, and/or on its worksheet 4562W, you are stuck with its ongoing tax basis accounting, year after year. You cannot take a depreciation allowance one year, and walk away from it the next year. Once an allowable deduction is claimed on Form 4562, the property item stays there until you properly dispose of it. A *disposition* means: full and adequate tax accounting.

Even after you recover all of your initial cost (and improvement costs) in a property item, you still leave it "on the books," if you continue to use the item in your business. By doing so, you justify the necessary expenditures for its repair, maintenance, and supplies. Staying on the books is required, whether it be listed property, Section 179 property, Section 280F property (50% or less business use), MACRS property, pre-MACRS property, or intangible property.

Once a property item has served its business purpose, or becomes old or obsolete, how do you get it off the books?

There are several ways. You can sell it; you can exchange it (trade it in); you can convert it to personal use; you can give it away; you can cannibalize it (remove the good parts); you can junk it; or you can destroy it. Whatever you do, you have to tax account for your actions. This means that you have to reveal and report on your return any attributable gain, loss, or wash that results.

So that you get the message more clearly, we depict in Figure 7.6 the *dispositional accounting* that is required. Note that this involves still another form, namely: **Form 4797**. This form is titled: *Sales or Exchanges of Business Property* (Including Involuntary Conversions and Recapture Amounts). Form 4797 is very comprehensive, and is beyond our discussion here. We just want you to be aware that it is a necessary adjunct to your tax return whenever you dispose of any depreciable asset.

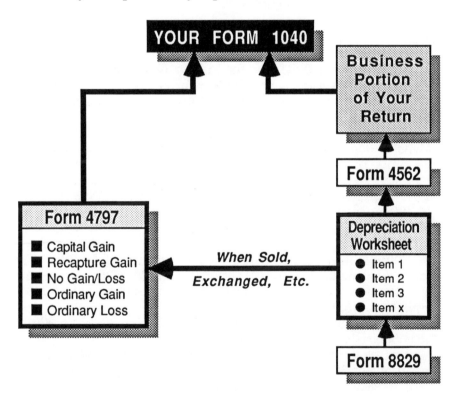

**Fig. 7.6 - Role of Form 4797 When Disposing of Business Assets**

Let us exemplify the dispositional accounting required. Suppose you purchased a 5-year class item of equipment for $23,650 (*not* an auto). You took the $10,000 Section 179 election, and you MACRS depreciated (at 200% DB) the $13,650 balance. At the end of three years, you disposed of the item. What is your cost recovery accounting situation?

At the end of three years, your unrecovered cost is $3,930. This derives from—

|  |  |  |
|---|---|---:|
| The Sec. 179 election |  | $10,000 |
| 1st yr | MACRS (20 % x $13,650) | 2,730 |
| 2nd yr | MACRS (32 % x  13,650) | 4,370 |
| 3rd yr | MACRS (19.2% x  13,650) | 2,620 |
|  |  | $19,720 |

[$23,650 initial cost less $19,720 recovered cost = $3,930 unrecovered cost.]

Suppose you sell the item for $6,000. Now what?

You have a taxable gain. The amount of gain is $2,070 [6,000 - 3,930]. It may consist of two parts: capital gain and recapture gain. The recapture gain is figured first.

Recapture gain is the amount by which the Section 179 and MACRS depreciation exceeds that of straight line depreciation for the period of use. In the example above, the amount of straight line depreciation would be $14,190 [($23,650 ÷ 5 yrs class life) x 3 yrs use]. Thus, the additional depreciation taken was $5,530 [19,720 - 14,190]. Recapture gain cannot exceed the actual gain, which in this case was $2,070. Hence, the actual gain is all recapture gain (which is treated as ordinary income).

Suppose the item sold for $10,000 instead of $6,000. The actual gain would be $6,070 [10,000 - 3,930]. Of this amount, $5,530 is recapture gain (from the computations above) and $540 is capital gain [6,070 - 5,530].

Suppose you sold the item for $2,000 instead of $6,000 or $10,000 as above. Now what happens?

You have a tax recognized loss. This is an ordinary loss to the extent of $1,930 (3,930 unrecovered basis - 2,000 sales price).

Similarly, you have to go through a dispositional accounting for every Form 4562 item that you want off the books. This is your opportunity to recover every penny of cost that you put into the property.

# 8

# SURVEILLANCE MATTERS

All Self-Employed Persons Are "Tax Suspect" And, Therefore, Are Kept Under Canvassing Surveillance. Because They Use The CASH METHOD Of Accounting, They Have More Opportunity Than Regularly Employed Persons To Underreport Income And Overclaim Deductions. When More Than $10,000 In Cash Is Received, Accumulated, Hoarded, Or Deposited, A 75-Question Form 8300 Is Required. Be Mindful Of The "Substantial Omission Rule" [Sec. 6501(e)(1)(A)] And Its 6-Year Examination Authority . . . For RECONSTRUCTION Of Income. Prepare Yourself For Special RESEARCH Audits Conducted On Selected Codified Businesses. The Results Are Used To "Profile Sweep" All Like Businesses In A Given IRS District.

The IRS would like nothing better than to eliminate all self-employed individuals, all independent contractors, and all nonemployees. It would much prefer to have all workers in the U.S. employed by only a handful of major corporations. This way, all money payments to persons could be centrally controlled, and all financial transactions by said persons would be dutifully reported to Big Brother by corporate entities.

In its peculiar mindset, the IRS views all independent persons as being engaged, at least to some degree, in the underground economy. It envisions that these persons, somehow, are hoarding billions of dollars of unreported income while simultaneously claiming grossly unallowable deductions on their tax returns.

You know, and we know, that this IRS fixation is false. It cannot eliminate all self-employed individuals; the so-called underground economy has limitations of its own; and not all business owners grossly overdeduct knowingly and maliciously. Nevertheless, the IRS continues to view most independent businesses with cynicism.

Consequently, in this chapter we want to try to pull together various surveillance matters which can adversely affect your business, if you are uninformed. These matters include the IRS's canvassing authority, its profiling programs, its cash/barter mania, its computer codification of business types, its reconstruction of income, its suspicions of your claiming purely personal expenditures as business deductions, and other authoritarian positions it takes to maximize revenue. Many of these matters are blindspots to newly self-employeds. Unless you are made aware of them in advance, you could suffer major tax and financial setbacks.

## Canvassing Authority

Many independent business owners are unaware of the vast surveillance and canvassing authority that the IRS has. This authority is used to gain income and expense information on targeted businesses without the owners ever knowing what is taking place. IRS canvassers screen catalog, sales, and other promotional literature, and use the information to stake out a business. They watch the goings and comings of customers, suppliers, workers, and the owner(s) thereof. The lifestyle of an owner is noted by the car he drives, his on- and off-duty hours, his manner of dress, where he lives, and where (and how often) he vacations. All of this is a form of government spying on its citizens. Its purpose, of course, is to glean an insight into those business operations that can produce maximum additional revenue.

The authority to canvass business operations is stated in Section 7601 of the IR Code. This section is titled: *Canvass of Districts for Taxable Persons and Objects*. Its subsection (a): General Rule, reads in full as follows:

> *The* [IRS District Director] *shall, to the extent he deems practicable, cause officers or employees of the* [IRS] *to proceed, from time to time, through each internal revenue district and inquire after and concerning all persons therein who may be liable to pay any internal revenue tax, and all persons owning or*

*having the care and management of any objects with respect to which any tax is imposed.*

If, after reading this Code section, there is any doubt in your mind about the IRS's surveillance authority, then you should read subsection (b): Penalties. This subsection reads in pertinent part as—

*Whoever corruptly or by force or threats of force (including any threatening letter of communication) endeavors to intimidate or impede . . . or obstructs or impedes . . . any officer or employee of the [IRS] acting in an official capacity . . . shall, upon conviction thereof, be fined not more than $5,000, or imprisoned not more than 3 years, or both . . . .*

We don't know about you, but whenever we read a tax law like this one, we boil under the skin. The IRS can threaten, intimidate, impede, and obstruct any business, and that's O.K. It can punch a computer key that sends out a threatening communication with penalty assessments, and that, too, is O.K. The IRS can enter your business premises at any time of the day, and at night when such premises are open [Sec. 7606]. Refusal to permit entry can subject the business owner to a $500 penalty . . . *for every such refusal.* All of this is hardly "a level playing field."

Our point is that the revenue laws are not written to inform you, nor to help you prosper in your business. They are written to threaten you with penalties, if you do not comply instantly with IRS demands. Said demands are often made on suspicion and whim: rarely on cold, hard, evidential facts. Your job, therefore, is to conduct your business in a legal, ethical, and above-board manner. Only in this way can tax suspicions of you, and tax demands on you, be minimized.

## "Cash Basis" Implications

Cash accounting is a perfectly legitimate method of keeping books and records for tax purposes. Section 446 makes this point very clear. Its subsection (a): General Rule, reads in full as—

*Taxable income shall be computed under the method of accounting on the basis of which the taxpayer regularly computes his income in keeping his books.*

Whereupon, subsection (c): Permissible Methods, says—

*A taxpayer may compute taxable income under any of the
following methods of accounting—*
  *(1)  the cash receipts and disbursements method;*
  [Emphasis added.]

Yet, when an IRS agent confronts a business owner, one of the
first inquiries that the agent makes pertains to one's method of
accounting.  The moment you respond by saying, "cash basis" or
"cash method," the agent waxes cynical. He/she starts making
sinister implications about your cash transactions.  A lot of personal
and probing questions are asked.  Some are legitimate, if they relate
expressly to the income reported on your return.  But many such
questions probe into your personal life and right of privacy.  For the
implicating questions, the term "cash" means coin and currency
(greenbacks) which are customarily accepted and used as money.
  Here are some typical cash-probing questions you may be asked:

1.  How much cash do you keep on hand in your business?
2.  How much cash do you carry on your person?
3.  How much cash does your spouse carry around, or have ready access to?
4.  How often do you tally your cash for your income records?  End of each
    day?  Week?  Month?
5.  Do you deposit the cash in your bank?  If so, how often?  Where are
    your deposit slips?
6.  Do you have a "cash hoard" among your personal savings?  If so, how
    much and why?

These and other questions are asked in a skewed manner that
implies that it is wrong to handle cash.  Pretty soon you start feeling
guilty.  Maybe you did stick a $10 bill or two in your pocket, to
make some petty cash purchases for your business or your family.
When you start getting nervous about this, the IRS smells blood and
bores in hard.  The questions are expanded to barter services and
property exchanges.  The implication is that you know that using
cash is wrong and, therefore, you have resorted to using substitutes
for cash.
  You have a right to use cash.  You have a right to keep a cash
hoard (under $10,000; we'll explain below).  You have a right to
receive cash, and a right to pay out cash.  So DO NOT let the IRS
con you out of these rights.

Make a concerted effort to record your cash income diligently. But, over the course of a year's time, if you forget to record a few hundred dollars — or even a few thousand — don't overworry about it. Do your best, of course, to correct it. You are not perfect . . . and neither is the IRS.

And don't let the IRS embarrass you with small cash inconsistencies. Once you are embarrassed, you tend to spill your beans and "confess everything." You then may say things that you should not have said, and which rarely have any bearing on your tax return. The IRS will never hold your confessions in confidence.

## Cash Over $10,000

The danger threshold for really suspicious behavior is $10,000. If, during the course of your trade or business, you receive and accumulate more than $10,000 in cash, and you take that over-$10,000 to the bank, guess what happens?

The bank, or other financial institution, has to fill out a special report on you, and forward it within 15 days to the IRS. The special report is Form 8300: *Report of Cash Payments Over $10,000 Received in a Trade or Business*. Its immediate subheading carries the official threat—

*Failure to file this form or filing a false form may result in imprisonment.*

This cash-over-$10,000 report is organized into four parts, namely:

Part I      — Identity of Individual From Whom the Cash Was Received
Part II     — Person on Whose Behalf This Transaction Was Conducted
Part III    — Description of Transaction and Method of Payment
Part IV     — Business Reporting This Transaction

The official instructions: Who Must File, say—

*Each person engaged in a trade or business who, during that trade or business, receives more than $10,000 in cash in one transaction or two or more related transactions, must file Form 8300. Any transactions conducted between a payer (or its agent)* *and the recipient in a 24-hour period are related transactions. Transactions are considered related even if they occur over a period of more than 24 hours if the recipient knows, or has reason to know, that each transaction is one of a series of connected transactions. This form may be filed voluntarily for any suspicious transaction, even if it does not exceed $10,000.*

Form 8300 contains approximately 75 line entries, a number of which have multiple subparts of their own. When you take your cumulative cash receipts to the bank, you have to endure the bank's close scrutiny. The obvious answer, of course, is: Do not take more than $10,000 to your bank at any one time.

Now, if you, in turn, receive more than $10,000 in cash from one or more related persons in one or more related transactions, you, too, have to prepare Form 8300 on that person or those persons. Part III of the form asks for the specific details listed in Figure 8.1. For this purpose, the term "cash" is expanded to include—

*a cashier's check, bank draft, traveler's check, or money order having a face amount of not more than $10,000 in a Designated Reporting Transaction* [a consumer durable, a collectible, a travel or entertainment activity], *or received in any transaction in which the recipient knows that such instrument is being used in an attempt to avoid the reporting of the transaction.*

The above should be sufficiently convincing to you that our system of taxation is based purely on the **assumption** that large transactions in cash are suspicious and possibly illegal.

## The 25% Omission Rule

Tax reportable income is that which is derived from business and other activities **throughout** the world. As a U.S. citizen or U.S. resident, you are required to report accountable income regardless of where it is derived: your local area, out of state, out of country. If you have foreign source income, it is usually taxed twice. It is taxed by the U.S. and also by the foreign situs country.

This "whatever source" requirement follows from Section 61: Gross Income Defined. Its subsection (a): General Definition, states—

| Part III | Report of Cash Payments Over $10,000 Received in a Trade or Business | Form 8300 |
|---|---|---|

### DESCRIPTION OF TRANSACTION AND METHOD OF PAYMENT

1. ☐ personal property
2. ☐ real property
3. ☐ personal services
4. ☐ business services
5. ☐ intangible property

6. ☐ debt obligations
7. ☐ exchange of cash
8. ☐ escrow or trust funds
9. ☐ other (specify)
..............................................
..............................................

10. Specific description of property or service purchased.
(serial no., registration no., parcel no., etc.)
..............................................

11. Total price in U.S. currency $............................

12. Amount U.S. currency received $............................

13. Amount in $100 bills or larger $ ..........................................................

14. Amount of cash received in other than U.S. currency. (Show exchange rate) $..........................................................

15. Specific description of cash received in other than U.S. currency
..........................................................
..........................................................

**Fig. 8.1 - Part III of the 75-Question Form 8300**

*Except as otherwise provided . . ., gross income means all income **from whatever source derived**, including (but not limited to) the following items:*
 *(1) Compensation for services;*
 *(2) Gross income from business;*
 *(3) Gains from dealings in property;*
 *. . . [etc. to (15)]* [Emphasis added.]
 *. . . [plus 20 more inclusions: Secs. 71-90].*

This definition is pretty all-sweeping. It is purposely intended to be. The intention is that **all** sources of income be tax accountable *. . . except as otherwise provided.* There are some 36 statutory exceptions (Sections 101 through 136). Some are very special, such as Section 136(a)(5): *Income derived from Federal Reserve banks, including capital stock and surplus* [owned by Federal Reserve Board members.] None of the exceptions favors self-employed businesses.

Because of the 36 statutory exceptions, there is genuine confusion as to what is meant by "all income from whatever source derived." As a result, when there is doubt, questionable income may be omitted. And in some cases, intentional calculated risks are taken (to omit income). If the omitted income could be disguised in some manner, perhaps, if discovered, it could be argued to be a variant of the many statutory exceptions. What we are getting at is this: Omissions of income, under any pretense, can expose a taxpayer to the 25% substantial omission rule of Section 6501(e)(1)(A).

The 25% omission rule says—

*If a taxpayer omits from gross income an amount properly includible therein which is in excess of 25 percent of the amount of gross income stated in the return, the tax may be assessed, or a proceeding in court for the collection of such tax may be begun without assessment, at any time within 6 years after the return was filed.*

Please read this carefully. The rule does **not** say that you are allowed to omit up to 25% of your business or personal gross income. The rule says that IF you omit more than 25%, up to six years of your tax returns can be examined. Ordinarily, the IRS has up to three years (after the April 15th due date) to examine your returns [Sec. 6501(a)]. If you file no return, assessment and collection of tax may proceed . . . *at any time* [Sec. 6501(c)(3)].

What happens if you omit income of less than 25%

That depends. If the omission was due to negligence, you are assessed the 20% accuracy penalty [Sec. 6662(a)]. If the omission was due to willfulness, you are assessed the 75% fraud penalty [Sec. 6663(a)]. All penalties are treated as *additions to tax.*

Obviously, omitting income, if detected, can cost you money.

## Reconstruction of Income

How does the IRS determine whether any business (or personal) income is omitted or not?

It does so by reconstructions, estimates, and — yes — pure speculation. If no return is filed, or if it is filed inaccurately, the IRS has reconstruction authority under Section 446 of the tax code.

Specifically, subsection 446(b): Exceptions [to methods of accounting], reads in full as—

*If no method of accounting has been regularly used by the taxpayer, or if the method used does not clearly reflect income, the computation of taxable income shall be made under such methods as, **in the opinion** of the* [IRS], *does clearly reflect income.* [Emphasis added.]

When you rely on the IRS to choose a reconstruction method that "clearly reflects income," you put your fate into irresponsible hands. The only obligation the IRS has is to make some computation that, in its opinion, is the "best evidence" of the omitted income. There is no requirement that the IRS be accurate or honest. This is the risk one takes for not reporting his income properly.

Any of at least six different methods can be used by the IRS for reconstructing income. These methods are:

1. Bank deposits analysis — all monies deposited are treated as taxable income.
2. Application of funds — all expenditures for the year are treated as taxable income.
3. Percentage markups — average industry markups are applied to changes in inventory to establish gross income.
4. Unit and volume estimates — undercover samplings of the total number of transactions per observational time.
5. Third party interviews — actual interrogations of customers, suppliers, and workers per average month.
6. Net worth computation — all increase in net worth for a target year is presumed to be taxable income.

Bear in mind that these are income *reconstruction* methods only. They are not everyday accepted accounting practices. Purposely, they establish overapproximations of income. It is then up to the business owner (taxpayer) to counter the IRS and prove it wrong. Again, this is the price you pay for inattention to proper income accounting methods.

## All Businesses Codified

The IRS has been in the tax collection business since 1913. That was when income taxation (via Amendment 16) first became constitutional. Over the years since then, the IRS has collected "tons" of confidential financial information on businesses of all types. It wasn't long before common trends and characteristics were noted in similar businesses. This commonness prompted the IRS to establish *tax profiles* of like businesses. These profiles in turn were used to select those business owners from whom extensive additional revenue could be wrung.

In 1982 (via the Tax Equity and Fiscal Responsibility Act), the IRS began codifying all businesses by **principal activity codes**. These codes are straight 4-digit numbers. Approximately 200 such 4-digit codes are used to classify businesses, large and small. These 200 or so codes are grouped (unevenly) into about 10 major categories. (See Figure 8.2.) In certain major categories, subcategories are indicated. For example, the major category designated as *Services: Personal, Professional, & Business*, has nine subcategories. The major category *Transportation Services* has no subcategories. The very last codified category is: *Unable to Classify*. It is signified as 8888 for proprietorships and as 8999 for partnerships.

Each business owner must select one 4-digit code number and enter it conspicuously on his tax return. The instructions for selection say—

*Locate the major category that best describes your activity. Within the major category, select the activity code that most closely identifies the business or profession that is the principal source of your sales or receipts. Enter this 4-digit code on page 1 [of the business portion of your tax return].*

There is no orderly system to the 4-digit assignments to each of the 200 or so business types. For proprietorships, particularly, the code assignments appear to be intentionally random. An astute taxpayer would have difficulty deciphering a code and reconstructing the profile specifics which the IRS has amassed for that type business.

The IRS uses the 4-digit code number for computer matching each business return with its data bank profile for the indicated type of business. The purpose in doing so is to detect those returns

| Approximately 200 4-Digit Code Numbers | |
|---|---|
| Agricultural Services, Forestry, Fishing | Real Estate |
| Construction<br>● Operative Builders<br>● Building Contractors<br>● General Contractors | Services: Personal, Professional, Business<br>● Amusement<br>● Automotive<br>● Business<br>● Personal<br>● Computer<br>● Hotels & Lodging<br>● Laundry and Cleaning<br>● Medical & Health<br>● Equipment Repair |
| Finance, Insurance, and Related Services | |
| Manufacturing, Printing, and Publishing | |
| Mining and Mineral Exploration | |
| Retail Trade - Selling Goods to Individuals and Households<br>● Catalog and Vending<br>● Apparel & Accessories<br>● Automotive & Services<br>● Hardware & Garden<br>● Food & Beverages<br>● Furniture & Merchandise<br>● Miscellaneous Retail | Wholesale Trade - Selling Goods to Other Businesses<br>● Durable Goods - Machinery, Equipment, Wood, Metals<br>● Nondurable Goods - Food, Fiber, Chemicals |
| | Transportation Services |
| | Unable to Classify |

**Fig. 8.2 - Principal Business Activities Codified by IRS**

which are "out of norm." An out-of-norm business return is one which has subnormal reported income and/or abnormal deductions and expenses. An out-of-norm return always excites the IRS because of the anticipation of more revenue.

## Special "Research" Audits

The bureaucracy reach of the IRS is never-ending. Its ongoing drive is to perfect its profiling of all codified businesses. To do this, every three to five years or so certain coded businesses are selected for special auditing. These are not routine audits; they are *research* audits.

The purpose of a research audit is to determine the latest trends and patterns in income reporting and claimed business expenses. In a routine audit, time is of the essence. In a research audit, IRS time is not of the essence. Whereas a small business owner may take three hours or so to prepare the business portion of his return (assuming that he has kept good records throughout the year), the research auditor may take anywhere from eight to 24 hours on the selectee's return. The term "research" means to review, probe, dig . . . and taunt the researcher.

Research auditing works this way. First, a particular business code group is selected for probing. For example, suppose an IRS "brain center" (there are 10 such regional processing centers throughout the U.S.) decides that insurance agents and brokers should be research probed. This taxpayer group is Code 5702 for proprietorships, and Code 6411 for partnerships. Then, a minimum of three separate 5702 (or 6411) businesses are selected. One reports relatively low gross income; one reports average gross income; and one reports relatively high gross income. The tax returns of the selected 5702 (or 6411) researchees are sent to a chosen IRS district (within the brain center's jurisdiction) with instructions for probing selected issues. The instructions include probing *three consecutive years*: target year, preceding year, and succeeding year. This general sampling technique, as we have observed it, is depicted in Figure 8.3. Senior field auditors are assigned to do the probing.

Suppose, for example, that the researcher found that the majority of 5702 researchees (insurance agents and brokers) claimed travel expenses for attending business conventions, foreign and domestic. In the first place, tax auditors inherently dislike taxpayers who attend business conventions. There is an element of personal envy here, as well as an opportunity for government agents to exert power over their taxpayer subjects. Besides the tax rules for attending conventions — Section 274(h) — are *very* stringent. Consequently, a research auditor can arbitrarily disallow all convention expenses and get away with it. Convention attendees rarely keep good records.

In a typical research audit, covering three years at a time, an aggressive auditor can net the IRS anywhere from $10,000 to $20,000 in additional revenue (per researchee). If an auditor spent 15 hours and assessed $15,000 in additional revenue, that would be a research return of $1,000 per hour. Not bad for a government agency bent on increasing its power.

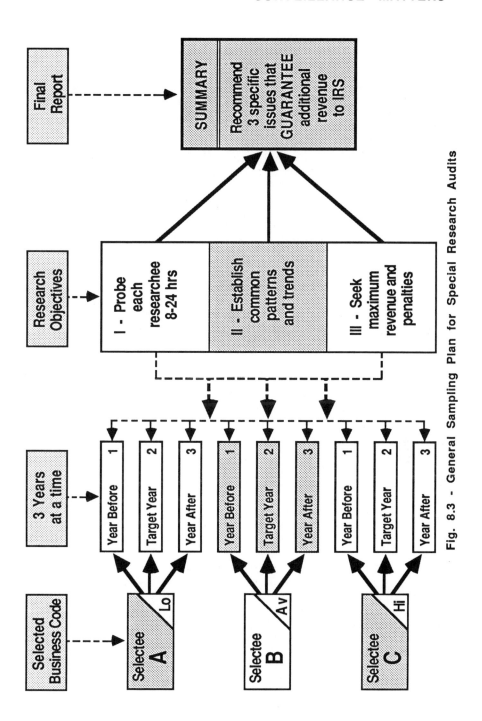

Fig. 8.3 - General Sampling Plan for Special Research Audits

## Profile Sweeping

Once the IRS tastes blood in its research of a selected business code, it goes for the jugular. If Code 5702 were the target, for example, it goes after all other 5702 returns in the same IRS district. The selectees are then set up for a "routine" audit, which lasts only one to two hours. In this short time, the IRS is guaranteed additional revenue collection because it already knows the key weaknesses of the selected business class. This is known as *profile sweeping*. It is a vacuum cleaner approach to all like businesses.

Each research auditor prepares a detailed report with specific revenue recommendations to his/her IRS supervisor. The district director transmits this information to the same service center from which the initial research instructions were issued. The district director also indicates the number of personnel locally assignable to the profile-sweeping effort. The service center uses the research reports for computer matching all like business in the reporting district. The center may pick 100, 200, 300 or more Code 5702 returns for a target year, and ship them to the local district for follow-up.

Suppose that an IRS district in a metropolitan area has 200 Code 5702 returns (insurance agents and brokers) sent to it. Suppose, also, that for each selectee (including prior- and subsequent-year returns), a conservative $5,000 in additional revenue (including penalties and interest) is assessed. And, further, suppose that each routine auditor spends, on average, two hours per auditee. Thus, in about 400 hours (200 selectees x 2 hrs each) the IRS would generate $1,000,000 ($1 million: 200 x $5,000) in additional revenue. With only five auditors assigned, for example, they could sweep in this amount in two weeks' time (5 x 40 hrs/wk x 2 wks = 400 hrs).

Now do you see the massive revenue benefit of profile sweeping?

The IRS has about 65 district offices strategically located through the U.S. If only one district can sweep in $1 million dollars in two weeks' time using five auditors, guess what happens? Other IRS districts are similarly instructed. The potential for sweeping in $65,000,000 every two weeks becomes irresistible.

Once one business code profile has been cleaned out, the IRS brain centers turn their surveillance attention to some other selected codified business. And so on . . . ad infinitum.

# 9

# NET PROFIT OR LOSS

Every Truly Self-Employed Seeks To Make A Profit By His/Her Material Participation In Business. Once Gross Income Is Established, The Net Profit Or Loss Is Determined By Some 20 To 30 Allowable Expense Deductions. The Statutory Standard For Allowability Is: ORDINARY AND NECESSARY . . . IN CARRYING ON One's Livelihood [IRC Sec. 162]. Personal Expenses Are Disallowed, Particularly When There Is Travel And Entertainment. If A Bona Fide Net Loss Is Incurred, It Is Allowed As An Offset Against Other Positive Sources Of Income On Form 1040. If 3 Loss Years In A 5-Year Period, The Business Is Presumed Not For Profit.

Every business entrepreneur seeks to make a net profit — the more the better. Well, . . . maybe it's not so better. The more net profit you make, the more income taxes you pay: both No. 1 **and** No. 2. In a convoluted way, perhaps, the more taxes you pay is an index of your success.

But should you show a net loss, your tax world changes. The biggest change is that, whereas the IRS covetously shares the biggest bite out of your success, it shuns sharing in your losses. A net loss in a given year implies to the IRS that somehow you are "fixing the books" to avoid taxes. So, naturally, stringent rules are imposed to make sure that your loss is bona fide. We'll tell you about the loss rules towards the end of this chapter.

In the meantime, we want to outline for you the coverage in this chapter. For this, we want to use Schedule C (Form 1040) as our roadmap and model. This tax form is officially titled: *Profit or Loss From Business (Sole Proprietorship)*. Unless you are involved in a partnership or farming, Schedule C (1040) is THE self-employment tax form to use. If you do not have an official copy of this form in your possession, we urge that you get one. We show you the general format of it in Figure 9.1.

| Sched.C (Form 1040) | PROFIT OR LOSS FROM BUSINESS | Tax Year |
|---|---|---|

Business name. Principal product or service. Accounting method. Inventory method. Check boxes. Activity code.

**Part I  INCOME**

Gross receipts, etc. ...............................................

Gross profit, etc. ...............................................

● GROSS INCOME ▶

**Part II  EXPENSES**

Advertising

● Etc.

● Etc.

Other expenses

● TOTAL EXPENSES ▶

Tentative profit or loss ...............................................

Business use of home ...............................................

■ NET PROFIT OR LOSS ▶▶▶

If a loss, MUST check (a) or (b)

(a) ☐ All at risk

(b) ☐ Some not at risk

*other "bottom line" instructions*

Fig. 9.1 - General Format of Page 1, Schedule C (Form 1040)

Schedule C (Form 1040) is a conventional profit-or-loss statement for any type of small business, be it a proprietorship, partnership, or even a corporation. It provides a good insight into the kinds of business expenses that are well recognized in the tax and financial world. It is the *expense deductions* that we want to focus on primarily. Other parts of the form are either self-explanatory, or we have touched on them previously.

After describing what is meant by "material participation" in your business, we want to start this chapter at the **gross profit** line on Schedule C. We discussed the sequence of events from gross receipts to gross profit back in Chapter 5: Direct Cost Items. We also summarized the sequence in Figure 5.1. Now, we want to move on.

## "Material Participation" Defined

A key element for recognizing any business expense deduction on Schedule C (1040) is the term: *material participation*. While this term may sound self-explanatory, in our IRS tax world, it is not. Unless one's participation in his/her self-employment business is "material," certain expenses are disallowed and any net loss is severely limited. The word "material" means more than passive.

The term "material participation" appears in subsections 469(c) and (h) of the Tax Code. The base Section 469 is titled: Passive Activity Losses Limited. It is in the definition of a passive activity that the term "material participation" first appears. Here, the exact statutory wording is—

Sec. 469(c)(1) — *The term "passive activity" means any activity*—
　*(A) which involves the conduct of any trade or business, and*
　*(B) in which the taxpayer does not materially participate.*

Sec. 469(h)(1) — *A taxpayer shall be treated as materially participating in any activity **only if** the taxpayer is involved in the operations of the activity on a basis which is*—
　*(A) **regular**,*
　*(B) **continuous**, and*
　*(C) **substantial**.* [Emphasis supplied.]

The three descriptive words above — *regular, continuous, substantial* — also appear self-explanatory. But the IRS, in its official instructions to Schedule C, uses over 500 words in seven "tests" to define material participation. The most succinct of the seven tests is Test 1 which says—

> *You materially participated in the operation of this trade or business activity . . . if . . . you participated in the activity for more than 500 hours during the tax year.*

In a normal 8-hour day, 5-day week, 50-week year, there are 2,000 hours of working activity. Many self-employeds work far more than this. So, 500 hours is easy qualifying time for meeting the material participation requirement.

Just before the income-reporting portion on Schedule C, a lead-off question reads:

> *Did you "materially participate" in the operation of this business during __(year)__ .* ☐ *Yes,* ☐ *No. (If "No" see instructions for limitation on losses.)*

Needless to say, our discussion in this entire book addresses only material participation in self-employed businesses.

## Adding "Other Income"

Previously, we stopped the income-reporting phase of Schedule C at the line designated as "gross profit." That is, gross receipts less returns and allowances, less cost of goods sold, equals gross profit. Now, we want to start with gross profit and move on down the Schedule C format in Figure 9.1.

If you look carefully at an *official* Schedule C (which Figure 9.1 is not), you will note that the term "gross profit *or loss*" does **not** appear. Yet, when you scan near the bottom of the official form, the term: "Net profit **or loss**" does appear. Obviously, if your gross profit is a loss, the rest of your Schedule C is virtually meaningless. Or, is it?

This is where the entry for "**other income**," if any, comes in. A negative gross profit (loss) can be meaningful if other income is added which makes the sum of the two positive.

On official Schedule C, other income is handled this way—

5. *Gross profit*          _____
6. *Other income*          _____
7. *Add lines 5 and 6*
   *This is your gross income* ==============

"What is this 'Other income' (line 6 above)?" you ask.

The simple answer is that it is not income (gross receipts or sales) that you generate regularly in your business. It comprises those various miscellaneous items that are treated as income when "associated with" or "related to" your material participation activities. This miscellany covers such items as—

  a.  occasional scrap sales
  b.  recovered bad debts
  c.  interest on accounts receivable
  d.  gas or fuel tax refunds
  e.  patronage dividends
  f.  inclusion amounts (leased autos)
  g.  charge backs (contingent sales)
  h.  referral fees
  i.  expense reimbursements
  j.  certain depreciation recapture
  k.  prizes and awards
  l.  legal judgments

. . . and other miscellaneous types of business-associated income that does not constitute the mainstream of your Schedule C daily activities.

If your "other income" produces a net profit to the business, said income is subject to the No. 2 tax as self-employment earnings. For this reason, it is important that you exercise care, and not report other income on Schedule C if it can be reported elsewhere on your return.

For example, suppose you have one or more business bank accounts that pay interest. This is a very common occurrence. Is this interest Schedule C income? Or, is it Schedule B income: Interest and Dividends?

It is Schedule B income. No No. 2 tax applies. Interest earned on depository accounts — *unlike* that earned on customer accounts receivable — is not business income. It is investment income. Different tax rules apply.

## Expense Deductions Overview

Once your gross income (which is gross profit plus other income) is entered on Schedule C, the subsequent items that influence your net profit or loss are your segregated expense deductions. There are approximately 20 different types of business expenses preprinted on the Schedule C. There is also room for hand-entering another six or so separate expenses which are distinctly applicable to your particular business.

When there are 20 to 30 business expense categories that are deductible, it is best that we first overview them all. Accordingly, a listing of such expenses (edited slightly) is presented in Figure 9.2. For our purposes, we have sequentially numbered the expenses starting with the very first entry that is preprinted on Schedule C. This is: *Advertising* [item 1]. The actual official line numbers, though sequentially numbered and sublettered, differ from those in Figure 9.2.

The Figure 9.2 listing of expenses derives directly from Section 162: ***Trade or Business Expenses***. Its subsection (a) reads in preamble as—

*There shall be allowed as a deduction all the **ordinary and necessary** expenses paid or incurred during the taxable year in carrying on any trade or business, including—* [Emphasis added.]

The word "including" is expanded more understandably in Regulation 1.162-1(a): Business Expenses in General. From this regulation, the most pertinent one-sentence excerpt is—

*Among the items included in business expenses are management expenses, commissions, labor, supplies, incidental repairs, operating expenses of automobiles in the trade or business, traveling expenses while away from home solely in the pursuit of a trade or business, advertising and other selling expenses, together with insurance premiums against fire, storm, theft, accident, or other similar losses in the case of a business, and rental for the use of business property.*

All of these items — and others — are expanded on more fully in about 25 more regulations. All of this regulatory detail focuses

| Listing of "Ordinary and Necessary" Business Expenses | |
| --- | --- |
| ● Edited  ● Explanations added  ● See Fig. 9.1, Part II | |
| **Item** | **Comment** |
| 1 . Advertising | including promotions & publicity |
| 2 . Bad debts | uncollectibles previously in income |
| 3 . Car & truck expenses | must attach with Form 4562 |
| 4 . Commissions & fees | paid to nonemployees ONLY |
| 5 . Depletion | for oil, gas, and mineral extraction |
| 6 . Depreciation | for wear, tear, obsolescence, etc. |
| 7 . Employee benefits | medical plans, dependent care, etc. |
| 8 . Insurance | casualty, liability, workers' comp. |
| 9 . Interest: Mortgage | for real property used in the business |
| 10. Interest: Other | for vehicles,machinery, equip.,etc. |
| 11. Legal & professional | attorneys, accountants, consultants |
| 12. Office expense | stationery, supplies, postage, etc. |
| 13. Pension & P/S plans | for qualified employees: NOT you |
| 14. Rent: vehicles & equip. | whether or not on lease |
| 15. Rent: buildings & storage | whether or not on lease |
| 16. Repairs & maintenance | to building, machinery, equip., etc. |
| 17. Supplies: general | materials, small tools, cartons, etc. |
| 18. Taxes & licenses | payroll, property, excise: NOT income |
| 19. Travel & lodging | when away overnight, airfare, etc. |
| 20. Meals & entertainment | less 20% disallowed |
| 21. Utilities & phone | electricity, water, trash, paging, etc. |
| 22. Wages | paid to employees ONLY |

→ OTHER EXPENSES:
    23. Amortization
    24. Prof. development
    25. Small gifts        } SEE TEXT
    26. Computer services
    27. Printing & photo
    28. Other

Total Expenses ▶ [          ]

Fig. 9.2 - Deductible Expense Items on Part II of Schedule C

squarely on the statutory concept of "ordinary and necessary" . . . when carrying on a trade or business.

Regulation 1.162-1(a) contains one very profound statement with which you should be cognizant. The statement reads—

*The full amount of the allowable deduction for ordinary and necessary expenses in carrying on a business is deductible, even though such expenses exceed the gross income derived during the taxable year from such business.* [Emphasis added.]

In other words, if an expense is allowable, the full amount is deductible **even if** it produces a net loss. We are telling you this upfront so that you won't "throttle back" on your deductions under the misconception that business losses are not allowed.

Nor should you steam full throttle ahead claiming every penny that you imagine to be a legitimate business expense. Prudence and due diligence are required down the entire listing of deductible expenses on your Schedule C.

## Some Practical Guidelines

In Figure 9.2, we list 28 categories of expense deductions which are candidate entries on Schedule C. Obviously, we cannot go through each one and cite all the pertinent tax rules and regulations . However, we can provide you with some practical guidelines for exercising diligence when making your own entries on Schedule C.

Right off, we'll tell you that an expense entry of less than $100 will rarely ever be questioned. Entries of more than $100 but less than $1,000 will seldom be questioned. It is not that those entries on Schedule C (Part II) of less than $1,000 are automatically allowed. It is just that on a tax schedule with 20 to 30 different expense deductions, there is more revenue potential in questioning amounts larger than $1,000.

If an expense entry is quite large, relative to your gross income, it is a virtual certainty that — sooner or later — it will be questioned by the IRS. What is "quite large"?

As a rule of thumb, if an expense entry is 25% or more of the amount of your gross income, it will be questioned. This means that when you make a large deduction entry, you are advised to have all of your backup documentation well organized and handy. Large deductions always stick out like distress beacons calling for attention. But, again, don't throttle back just because a deduction is large. Do your homework and prepare to stand your ground.

Certain expense items, by their very nature, are almost always questioned. These are such items as car and truck expenses, leased luxury autos, depreciation of listed property, and travel and entertainment. Not only are the tax rules on these items tricky and restrictive, there is temptation — especially for self-employeds — to disguise some of their personal expenses as business expenses. This is an area where your accounting self-discipline is put to its ultimate test.

Even without personal-use problems, transportation vehicles, machinery and equipment, and real estate used in business are frequently questioned. This is because they are multi-year items. If you screw up in one year (the questioned year), you probably screwed up the year prior and the year after. So, make sure that you are on solid ground when you claim depreciation-type (multi-year) expenses. Recall Chapter 7: Depreciation, Etc., in this regard.

### Personal Expenses:   No-No

For self-employeds, particularly, the IRS is paranoid on personal expenses. This is one area of tax law where the basic rule is quite clear. *No personal, living, or family expenses . . . shall be allowed* (period)! [IRC Sec. 262(a).]

Unfortunately, the IRS tends to be aggressive and overbearing in its interpretation of this law. Agents and examiners too often base their disallowance assertions on conjecture and whim, rather than on the particular facts of each case. Unfortunately, also, they rarely read — and rarely comprehend — the IRS's own regulations which are intended to clarify matters.

On particular point is Regulation 1.262-1(b): *Examples of personal, living, and family expenses.* This regulation lists nine examples of the types of expenses expressly disallowed, namely—

(1)   Premiums paid for life insurance by the insured.
(2)   Insurance on a dwelling owned and occupied by the taxpayer.
(3)   Expenses for maintaining a family household.
(4)   Losses upon sale or other disposition of a personal residence.
(5)   Travel and entertainment unless qualified as business.
(6)   Breach of promise to marry and attorney fees therewith.
(7)   Legal and other costs in connection with divorce, separation, etc.
(8)   Uniforms and equipment to the extent of nontaxable allowances.
(9)   Education expenses, unless primarily for business.

In addition, Regulation 1.262-1(c) lists 10 cross references to other sections of the tax code. These cross references specify those personal-type expenses which are (partially) deductible on Schedule A (Itemized Deductions), but NOT on Schedule C. These 10 Code sections are—

  (1)   Sec. 163 (interest: especially mortgage interest)
  (2)   Sec. 164 (taxes: particularly property taxes)
  (3)   Sec. 165 (casualty losses and thefts)
  (4)   Sec. 166 (nonbusiness bad debts)
  (5)   Sec. 170 (charitable contributions and gifts)
  (6)   Sec. 213 (medical and dental expenses)
  (7)   Sec. 214 (expenses for certain dependent care)
  (8)   Sec. 215 (alimony and spousal support)
  (9)   Sec. 216 (taxes and interest for co-op housing)
 (10)   Sec. 217 (moving expenses for new job)

There is a point that we are trying to get across here. It is that while pure personal expenses are flat out disallowed, there are certain exceptions and certain conditions where some of the expenses are indeed allowed. The exceptions apply when a bona fide business purpose is served. So, be sure to read Regulation 1.262-1 with care. Read "between its lines" for the acceptable business connotations.

## The Capitalization Craze

We introduced the IRS's "capitalization craze" back in Chapter 3: Keeping Proper Records. We pointed out then that if the IRS can force you to capitalize an item which you claim as an expenses, two things happen. One, your No. 1 and No. 2 taxes are increased. And, two, your operating cash (cash flow) is reduced. This is a bad situation for any small business.

Thus, when you enter your paid expenses on Schedule C, the IRS may — and often does — come along several years later and tries to recharacterize some of your expense entries. For this, the principal expense targets are:

  (a)   Office expenses
  (b)   Repairs & maintenance
  (c)   Supplies & small tools

Should any of these items come under scrutiny, you will be asked to provide *all* of your purchase invoices for each of these line entries. The IRS will pick its way through your stack and pluck out all invoices that exceed $100. Next, it will go through each plucked invoice looking for single items that exceed $100. Then you will be asked: "How long will the $100-plus item last?"

The IRS still today uses an outmoded rule of thumb that says, "If an item costs more than $100 and will last more than one year" it has to be capitalized. For example, if you bought an electrical cable that hooks up to your computer, and it cost $101.15, the IRS wants you to capitalize it over five years. Similarly, if you bought an electric hand drill for shop use, and it cost $102.25, it, too, would have to be depreciated over five years. Yes, we know; this is ridiculous. But this is the mindset of revenue sleuths.

In any trade or business, materials, supplies, and small tools are deductible . . . *only in the amount that they are actually consumed and used in operation during the taxable year* [Reg. 1.162-3].

What happens when there are materials and supplies on hand at the end of the year and not consumed? You are supposed to include them in inventory or on your depreciation schedules. However, if you can show that you consistently replace the items as they are consumed, you can continue to expense them.

Repair and maintenance items constitute an age-old argument with the IRS. Most instructive for you is Regulation 1.162-4. Its principal points are—

*The cost of incidental repairs which **neither materially add to the value of the property nor appreciably prolong** its life, but keep it in an ordinarily efficient operating condition, may be deducted as an expense. . . . Repairs in the nature of replacements, to the extent that **they arrest deterioration and appreciably prolong the life** of the property, shall be capitalized and depreciated.* [Emphasis added.]

What is a "material addition" to the value of property? Is it $100 as the IRS insists? A $100 electrical cable added to a $10,000 computer is **not** a material addition, regardless of what the IRS says. Furthermore, said cable will not appreciably prolong the computer's life, even though the cable itself may last more than one year. Why is common sense so often missing in the IRS?

## Travel and Entertainment

There is one expense category that you probably should throttle back on. This pertains to travel and entertainment. Here, the term "travel" means away from home overnight; the term "entertainment" includes meals. Self-employment persons are vulnerable to accusations of engaging in unnecessary travel and in lavish entertainment. The substantiation rules (recordkeeping) on these matters — Section 274: Disallowance of Certain Entertainment, Etc. Expenses — are incredibly complex. You'll spend recordkeeping time that is far out of proportion to any deduction benefits that you might derive.

We exclude car and truck expenses from this "throttle back" advice. Car and truck expenses are regarded as local transportation matters. The business necessity for this type of expense is more easily established. Overnight lodging is not involved, and entertainment (if any) is minimal and inexpensive.

But if travel (away overnight) is truly necessary and solely for business purposes, it is deductible . . . and should be claimed. In this regard, Regulation 1.162-2(a) says quite clearly that—

*Traveling expenses include travel fares, meals and lodging, and expenses incident to travel such as expenses for sample rooms, telephone and telegraph, public stenographers, etc. Only such traveling expenses as are **reasonable and necessary** in the conduct of the taxpayer's business and **directly attributable** to it may be deducted.* [Emphasis added.]

In case of your spouse or other family member accompanying you on a business trip, Regulation 1.162-2(c) says—

*Where a taxpayer's wife accompanies him on a business trip, expenses attributable to her travel are **not** deductible unless it can be adequately shown that the wife's presence . . . has a bona fide business purpose. The wife's performance of some incidental service does **not** cause her expenses to qualify as deductible business expenses. The same rules apply to any other member of the taxpayer's family who accompany him on such a trip.* [Emphasis added.]

The message here is clear. Don't expect to take your spouse and children on a family vacation and try to write the whole affair off as a business trip. Don't even try. If you perform some incidental bona fide business function while on such a trip, claim *only* that incidental expense. Nothing more.

### Employing Own Children

Taking your children on a business trip is a "No-No" for expense deduction purposes. But there is nothing wrong with *employing* your children in your business. There is no law against it. Small businesses employ children — especially teenagers — all the time. As long as child labor laws are not violated, there's no tax prohibition against engaging persons who are legal minors.

In the case of your *own* children, however, certain tax precautions are required. Foremost is a written job description for each son or daughter (or grandson or granddaughter) that you employ. Secondly, you make sure that each child actually does the work that he or she is assigned to do. And, thirdly, you need to keep more accurate time records on your own children than you need for other workers: employees and nonemployees.

With your own children, there is always the suspicion that you are putting them on the payroll for the sole purpose of diluting and decreasing your taxable income from the business. This suspicion is aggravated when you pay your son or daughter an hourly rate that is distinctly higher than the industry average in your area. The only way to allay this suspicion is by being more insistent with your own children than you might be with other people's children. Pay the same hourly rate that you'd pay someone else's children.

The best tactic to use is to engage your children as employees until each one reaches age 18. Then switch them over to nonemployee status after age 18. The reason for this is that children employed in a family business are *exempt* from social security and medicare tax until age 18 [Sec. 1402(c)(2)(A)].

After age 18, whether your child is an employee or nonemployee, the social security/medicare tax applies. Chances are, though, by the time your child reaches age 20 or so, he or she will be seeking greater independence from you as a parent. Consequently, you might as well keep each child on as an employee until his/her active interest in your business naturally wanes.

Unmarried children, earning less than $6,000 pay little or no *income* tax. Therefore, if you pay each of your children $6,000 for the year, you reduce the taxable income from the business by the same amount. This is like drawing $6,000 tax free (per child) out of the business. There is nothing wrong with this so long as you enter the amount of gross wages paid on your Schedule C (at line 22, *Wages*, in Figure 9.2). You also have to prepare the proper employer returns and Form(s) W-2.

### Other Expenses: Various

On Schedule C, Part II, there is a preprinted expense entry titled: *Other expenses (list type and amount)*. Six blank lines follow. These enable you to enter those expenses which are significant to your business, but which are not otherwise characterized by the preprinted lines on the official form. In Figure 9.2, we used five of the six lines for example purposes.

On line 23 in Figure 9.2, we listed *Amortization* as the first example of "other expenses." If you recall from Chapter 7 (the section headed: Amortizing Intangibles), you initially enter your amortization allowance(s) on Form 4562: Depreciation and Amortization. The instructions on Form 4562 tell you to enter the allowable amount . . . *on the "other expenses" line of your return.*

We also listed in Figure 9.2 the example item: *Prof. development* for "professional development." This is the preferred tax terminology when incurring business expenses for educational courses, attending seminars, and taking field trips for—

(a)  maintaining or improving skills in your **existing** trade, business, or profession; or

(b)  meeting the requirements of applicable law or regulation for **retaining your license** "to practice," whatever your trade or business.

Educational expenses that qualify you for a new trade or business are not deductible.

The third other-expense item we listed in Figure 9.2 is: *Small gifts*. These are the customary business costs for "promoting goodwill." Caution is required because of the adjective "small." As per Section 274(b), no deduction is allowed for gifts which exceed $25 per business person per year. Of course, you can make gifts of greater value, but the excess over $25 is regarded as a personal expense. This rule applies to personal consumption gifts such as food, flowers, drinks, cosmetics, etc. If you give tickets to sports, musical, or theatrical events, these come under the heading of "Entertainment" where a 20% disallowance rule applies.

Another item that is often entered as an other expense is: *Computer services*. These are fees and costs that you might pay to consultants, trouble shooters, freelance operators, and outside computing services. Still other items might be: contract services, printing and photocopying, postage and freight, dues and publications, uniforms, laundry and cleaning, replacement tools, alarm system, and so on.

Almost every business has a special category or two (or three) of expense items which do not fit appropriately into the preprinted expense lines on Schedule C. This is where the "Other expense" blank lines come in handy.

### Tentative Profit (Loss)

Schedule C, Part II: Expenses, can accommodate up to 28 entry items. Because of this large number, it is inadvisable to add nonform attachments which list additional expense items. Stick to the preprinted lines as much as possible, and use the other expense lines as necessary.

Above all, do not attach your own computerized business expense spreadsheet. The IRS tends to ignore all attachments which are not specifically called for on the face of Schedule C itself. Actually, only three attachments are called for (if applicable), namely:

Form 4562 — Depreciation and Amortization
Form 8829 — Business Use of Home
Form 6198 — At-Risk Limitations

If you attach anything else, it can be detached and thrown away. This is the consequence of the so-called "Paperwork Reduction Act." Now you know why, at the very bottom of every official tax form, there is a small-print bold notation that reads: *For Paperwork Reduction Act Notice, see Form 1040 instructions*. This is put there to warn you: Don't attach unnecessary paper.

Once all of your business expenses are properly entered, your next job is to total them. The instructions say—

*Add the amounts in lines _____ through _____. These are your **total expenses** before expenses for business use of your home.*

Next comes your **tentative** profit (or loss). To determine this amount, you subtract your total expenses from your gross income. The sequence is—

Step 1 — Gross income
Step 2 — Total expenses
Step 3 — Subtract step 2 from step 1
= Tentative profit (loss)

There are two reasons for this tentative profit/loss line. One is to give you a chance to review all of your Schedule C entries before finalizing the bottom line. Secondly, it is to require you to complete Form 8829: Business Use of Your Home, if it is applicable. If it is applicable, you have to again review your expense items to see that there is no duplication of the same amounts on both Schedule C *and* Form 8829. We discussed Form 8829 and its expense entries in Chapter 4, and so we will not repeat them here.

And, finally, comes your net profit or net loss. This is obtained by subtracting Form 8829 expenses from your tentative profit or tentative loss.

As a summary and review of he key sequential steps to this point, we present Figure 9.3. Note that we start at your gross receipts and proceed on down to your net profit or net loss. This is your "bottom line" on Schedule C. Your net profit or loss is subsequently entered on page 1 of your Form 1040, where it combines with other income or losses you may have.

## What If Net Loss

If you have a net profit from your business, that's fine. You share it with the IRS via its Tax No. 1 and its Tax No. 2. But what if you have a loss? Will the IRS share this with you?

Yes, to some extent. That is, to the extent of *your* financial risk in the activity. The IRS never risks anything in any business. You know this. All entrepreneurial risk is at your expense.

Immediately below the bottom line: **Net profit or loss** on Schedule C, the following instruction appears:

*If you have a loss, you MUST check the box that describes your investment in this activity:*

(a) ☐ *All investment is at risk*

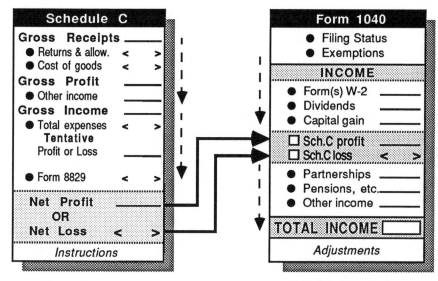

**Fig. 9.3 - Sequence of Entries: Schedule C to Form 1040**

    *(b)* ☐ *Some investment is not at risk*
*If you checked (a), enter the loss on Form 1040.*
*If you checked (b), you MUST attach Form 6198.*

What is this "at risk" check-boxing all about?

It's about Section 465 of the Tax Code. This section is titled: **Deductions Limited to Amount at Risk.** It takes over 6,000 words of tax law to tell you what is meant by "at risk." We will give you the core gist of it.

Basically, you are at risk for those investment amounts in your business which represent—

    1.    Your contributions in cash and other property.
    2.    Any money you borrow and for which you are personally liable for repayment.
    3.    Any property you own that you pledge to the extent of its fair market value.

In contrast, you are **not** at risk if you—

    (1)    Borrow money (for the business) from a related person.

(2)   Borrow money from a person who has a financial interest in the business.

(3)   Borrow money which is . . . *protected against loss through nonrecourse financing, guarantees, stop loss agreements, or other similar arrangements* [Sec. 465(b)(4)].

In other words, if you borrow money for which — either formally or informally — you are "protected" against repayment in the event of a business loss, you get no tax deduction for such loss. That is, your amount of Schedule C loss is limited strictly to the amount of money that you personally have at risk in the business. This is what Form 6198: At-Risk Limitations, is all about.

Rarely is any self-employed person able to borrow money from others, knowing in advance that the money does not have to be paid back in the event of a business loss. Consequently, be sure to check box (a) [All investment is at risk] and follow the instructions for completing your return.

### Effect of Loss on Form 1040

The Schedule C instructions for the at-risk box (a) say—

*If you checked (a), enter the loss on Form 1040, line _____.*

This means that your net loss is tax allowed in full.

A Schedule C net loss is treated as income — albeit negative — on page 1 of Form 1040 (U.S. Individual Income Tax Return). There it combines with 15 other items of income — business, nonbusiness, and personal — that you have for the year.

The specific line where the above entry is made is identified by the wording—

*Business income or (loss) (attach Schedule C)* _$<_____>_ .

The parentheses around the word "loss" are to signify that if the amount is indeed a loss, you are to indicate it as such with either angle brackets < > or parentheses ( ) around the entered columnar amount.

When the net loss from Schedule C combines with the 15 other items of income, some of which themselves may be negative, you arrive at your **total income** for the taxable year. (You might want

NET PROFIT OR LOSS

to glance at Figure 9.3 again.) In the great majority of cases, the total income on Form 1040 is a positive amount. This is so even when the negative Schedule C amount is included.

But there are times when the total income on Form 1040 may itself turn out to be a negative number (meaning a loss). In this case, you have what is called: a *tentative* Net Operating Loss (NOL). When determined computationally correct, an NOL becomes a recognized tax **deduction**. It may be deducted on prior-year returns, or on subsequent-year returns. It is not deductible on the current year return because, once you have an NOL, there is zero regular income tax. One cannot reduce his tax below zero. Therefore, an NOL is either carried back or carried forward.

The NOL rules are set forth in Section 172: *Net Operating Loss Deduction*. This is a 5,500-word tax law. Its gist is that if you compute the NOL correctly, you can carry it back three years, then carry it forward up to 15 years following the taxable year of the loss. To compute the NOL properly, you have to use Schedule A, Form 1045: Computation of NOL.

If you do not want to use the NOL computational form, you may forego the carryback option and use the tentative NOL for carry-forward only. This is sanctioned by subsection 172(b)(3): *Election to Waive Carryback*. If you elect to do this, you have to indicate your intention on the current loss year return. For this, there is some columnar white space on Form 1040, just below the line entry which reads: *Total income*. If this is a negative amount, place brackets (or parentheses) around it and mark it: **NOL**. Then hand-print the following notation in the columnar white space [T/P = taxpayer]:

T/P waives carryback & elects carryforward: IRC Sec. 172(b)(3)

This way, on your subsequent-year return (page 1 of Form 1040), you enter the NOL carryforward on the very last preprinted income line. This line reads—

*Other income (list type and amount)* ...........................

On the dotted line provided, enter: NOL carryforward: Sec. 172(b)(3). Then in the adjacent columnar space, enter the dollar amount with either brackets < > or parentheses ( ).

## What If Consecutive Losses

As a truly self-employed individual, you're in business to make a profit: not a loss. But if it is your first year, you may not make a net profit. This is tax acceptable. In many new businesses, a first-year loss is to be expected.

Suppose you incur a net loss in the second year of your business. That, too, is tax acceptable.

But, what if you make a Schedule C loss three consecutive years in a row? What are the tax consequences, if any?

In the first place, if you incur a loss three years in a row, you probably should not be self-employed. Or, at least, you should not be self-employed in that particular business. After all, irrespective of the tax consequences, you cannot expect to derive a livelihood if your profit/loss bottom line is consistently negative.

As to the tax consequences, the IRS comes along and invokes Section 183 against you. This section: *Activities Not Engaged in For Profit*, says that — unless you can show good reasons to the contrary — your total business deductions cannot exceed your business gross income. In other words, your bottom line on Schedule C is neither a profit . . . nor a loss. It is *zero*. This prevents an otherwise net loss from being used to offset any of your other sources of positive income on Form 1040. The net, net effect is that there is no further NOL carryforward deduction.

Section 183 invokes what is called: *a statutory presumption*. The presumption is that if you do not make a net profit in any three out of five consecutive years of doing business, you are in business for hobby reasons: not for livelihood reasons. Tax technically, you are allowed two loss years in any five years of business. Come the third loss year, your motives become suspect. It is presumed that you are not in business for profit reasons.

If your business looks like you are on the verge of breaking out of the financial doldrums, you CAN OVERRIDE the Section 183 presumption. To do so, however, you have to pass the IRS's "Nine Tests of Relevance" [Reg. 1.183-2(b)].

The nine tests are designed to flush out your intent to improve profitability. You can do this by showing that you are devoting most — if not all — of your personal time and energy to the business, and that in doing so, there is little, if any, personal pleasure or recreation involved. Enjoyment when making a loss is a clear giveaway. But if your business is profitable, there is nothing wrong with deriving pleasure and enjoyment therefrom.

# 10

# SE AND ES TAXES

The Self-Employment (SE) Tax Is Sacrosanct
. . . And Irreducible. You Compute It By Using
Schedule SE: Short Or Long. There You
Combine Your Profits And Losses From
Schedules C, F, And K-1, And Apply A 12.4%
Rate For Social Security And A 2.9% Rate For
Medicare. Separate Schedules SE Are
Required For Husband And Wife. The
Combined SE Tax Is Entered On Form 1040,
Page 2, And 50% Is Entered On Page 1. On
April 15, You Commence PREPAYING
Estimated (ES) Tax For The Current Year.
Normally, 4 ES Payment-Vouchers Are
Required. Only 3 Are Required If You File (And
Pay) Your Annual Form 1040 On Or Before
January 31 Each Year.

The letters "SE" stand for Self-Employment (tax); the letters "ES" stand for Estimated (tax). The SE tax is the No. 2 tax that we described quite extensively in Chapter 2. The ES tax is a combination of the No. 1 and No. 2 taxes for which *prepayment in advance* is required. Neither the SE tax nor the ES tax can be determined until the end of the taxable year for which your overall return — Form 1040 and its attachments — is prepared.

When self-employed, one particular attachment to Form 1040 is Schedule SE: *Self-Employment Tax*. There are several tricky computational aspects to this tax that we want to tell you about. For example, if you are married, the SE tax is NOT a joint tax as is the No. 1 tax. For distinguishing between the two, the No. 1 tax is often referred to as the "filing status" (or regular) tax. The tax rates and amount of tax you pay differ, depending on whether you file as single, married joint, married separate, head of household, or widow(er) with dependent child. There is no such variation in the No. 2 tax. It is a one-tax-rate tax for all self-employeds, regardless of filing status.

The SE tax actually has two components: Social Security and Medicare. Figuring these two components adds complications to Schedule SE. There are also complications when you work as an employee while being self-employed in the same year.

The ES tax is a four-times-a-year prepayment of your upcoming tax. If your estimated total tax (No. 1, No. 2, and any other) exceeds $500, the ES tax is mandatory. Because you are only allowed a 10% tolerance for being off your estimate, the four estimates a year can be a nightmare. This is especially true for self-employeds whose net earnings are seldom uniform, nor always predictable in the forthcoming year. But we'll have some practical suggestions for you in this regard.

Because the SE and ES taxes go hand in hand, we discuss them both in this chapter. Fully employed persons rarely have to worry about either of these taxes. Usually, the employer takes care of such matters through withholdings.

## A "Per Worker" Tax

Our Social Security System is based on the sole premise that, for each worker, there is a *centralized earnings record* for that one worker alone. Said government recordkeeping is required, whether the worker is 10 years old or 100 years old . . . and still working. Whether employed or self-employed, each worker's earnings are his or her own. There is no commingling of this recordkeeping between spouses and other close family members. Each worker is assigned his/her own social security account.

It is this "per worker" concept that is the focus of Schedule SE. This is quite evident in its first two entry spaces. The first entry space reads—

*Name of person with **self-employment** income (as shown on Form 1040)*

Note that this entry does NOT say: *Name(s) shown on Form 1040*, as does every other schedule or form which attaches to the 1040. Thus, if you are a self-employed worker, your name only goes on

Schedule SE. If you are married and file Form 1040 jointly, take care not to include your spouse's name.

The second entry space on Schedule SE is—

*Social security number of person with self-employment income* ▶ _____|__|_____

Note particularly that it is your social security number (SSN) that is asked for. It is NOT your EIN (Employer ID number) that you may have used on Schedule C. If you intentionally want to foul the system up, enter your EIN instead of your SSN. Within a few years, you'll have both the IRS and SSA (Social Security Administration) on your back.

Most foul-ups occur inadvertently between spousal social security numbers when filing a joint return. If the husband is self-employed, and the wife is not, there is seldom any SSN mixup. But if the wife is self-employed, and the husband is not, transposition often occurs because the husband's SSN usually appears first on Form 1040. When both spouses are self-employed, transposition of the wife's SSN on the husband's Schedule SE, and of the husband's SSN on the wife's Schedule SE are common.

To help you visualize the preparatory care required when both spouses are self-employed, we present Figure 10.1. Can you imagine what happens when husband and wife are in the same self-employment business together, and they agree to alternate the years for which they file separate Schedules SE?

## Schedules C, F, & K-1

Before we tell you about the computational aspects of Schedule SE, we need to go back and look at its predecessor self-employment earnings computations. There are three particular schedules that we have in mind, only one of which you are aware of at this point. These tax schedules are: Schedule C (Form 1040), Schedule F (Form 1040), and Schedule K-1 (Form 1065). The Schedule C is for nonfarm proprietorships; the Schedule F is for farm proprietorships; the Schedule K-1 is for partnerships, farm and nonfarm. The bottom line instruction to each of these schedules directs you onto Schedule SE.

Below the net profit or loss line on Schedule C, the specific instructions read—

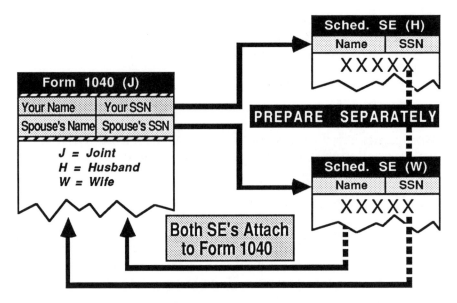

**Fig. 10.1 - Name and SSN Care When preparing Schedule(s) SE**

*If a profit . . . enter the net profit on Schedule SE, line _____.*

*If a loss . . .* [and] *you checked box (a)* [All investment is at risk], *enter the loss on Schedule SE, line _____.*

Whether your Schedule C self-employment earnings are a net profit or a net loss, you enter the amount on Schedule SE. If you show a loss, and you have no other self-employment activity for the loss year, Schedule SE would serve no purpose. There'd be no No. 2 tax. But since Schedule SE encompasses all self-employment activities, one or more of them may indeed show a profit. Because of this possibility, loss amounts are transferred to Schedule SE as well as profit amounts.

Schedule F: Profit or Loss from Farming, is used by self-employed farmers, fishermen, ranchers, orchardists, and vineyard operators. The Schedule F format is quite similar to that of Schedule C. The preprinted income and expense categories on Schedule F are similar to, but different from, those on Schedule C. Otherwise, the bottom line is the same: net farm profit or loss. The instructions at the Schedule F profit/loss line are identical to those on Schedule C above.

Schedule K-1 (Form 1065) carries the title: Partner's Share of Income, Credits, Deductions, Etc. Form 1065 itself is titled: U.S. Partnership Return of Income. Whether one is in a farm or nonfarm partnership, the tax forms are the same. As defined in the 1065 instructions—

*A partnership is the relationship between two or more persons who join to carry on a trade or business, with each person contributing money, property, labor, or skill and each expecting to share in the profits and losses of the business whether or not a formal partnership agreement is made.*

Now do you sense the virtues (?) of Schedule SE? The profits and losses from three basic types of self-employment business (Schedules C, F, and K-1) can be added together, to come up with a net, net profit or a net, net loss. If the result is a net, net loss from multiple businesses, you do not need to file Schedule SE.

There are two versions of Schedule SE: a *short* and a *long*. The short Schedule SE is for workers who are self-employed (only) in one or more businesses. The long Schedule SE is for workers who are both employed and self-employed in two or more (separate) businesses.

**The "Short" Schedule SE**

The short form of Schedule SE: Self-Employment Tax, is actually short. It consists of just five lines. It can be used only where a worker's net, net earnings (from one or more businesses) is derived from Schedule C, Schedule F, or Schedule K-1, or from any combination thereof. If employee-type earnings are involved, the "long" Schedule SE has to be used.

The short Schedule SE is self-contained and self-explanatory. Its simple format and five entry lines are presented in Figure 10.2. It's the fifth line — computation of the SE tax — that causes some confusion. Let us explain.

The SE tax — the No. 2 tax — is a *social* tax. It consists of two components: social security (for old-age, survivor's, and disability insurance) and medicare (for hospitalization insurance). Being a social tax, its rate and earnings base for computational purposes changes (increases) from year to year. As part of the original mandate in 1935, when the Social Security Act was enacted, the No. 2 tax must keep pace with the actuarial needs of the elderly and the

| Sched. SE (Form 1040) | Self-Employment Tax | Tax Year |
|---|---|---|
| **Your Name** | | **Your SSN** |

*General Instructions*

**SECTION A - SHORT FORM**

| | | |
|---|---|---|
| **1** | Net profit or loss from Schedule C and from Schedule K-1 (Form 1065) | |
| **2** | Net profit or loss from Schedule F and from Schedule K-1 (Form 1065) | |
| **3** | Combine lines 1 and 2 | |
| **4** | Multiply line by 0.9235. If result LESS THAN $400, do not file this schedule. You DO NOT owe SE tax. | |

Otherwise, line 4 is your SE Net Earnings

| | | |
|---|---|---|
| **5** | If amount on line 4 is -<br>● $55,500 or less, multiply by 0.153<br><br>● Over $55,500 but less than $130,200 multiply excess of $55,500 by 0.029 and add $8,491.50 (for 1992)<br><br>● $130,200 or more, enter $10,657.80 | |

The amount on line 5 is your SE Tax

☐ Enter 50% of line 5 on Form 1040, **Page 1.**
☐ Enter 100% of line 5 on Form 1040, **Page 2.**

**Fig. 10.2 - The Short Schedule SE with Instructions Abbreviated**

sick of America. The result is that this No. 2 tax is sacrosanct. It is politically untouchable . . . and irreducible.

For Figure 10.2 line 5 purposes, we use 1992 as our reference year. For 1992, the social security component of the SE tax is—

12.4% of net earnings up to $55,500.

Correspondingly, the medicare component is—

2.9% of net earnings up to $130,200.

The sum of these two percentages is 15.3% (for 1992).

As a historical note, the No. 2 tax for self-employeds was first imposed in 1954. The rate then was just 3% of net earnings up to $1,600. Compare the difference some 40 years later!

With this background, the preprinted instructions to line 5 on short Schedule SE read as follows:

*If the amount on line 4 is—*

> *(A) $55,500 or less, multiply line 4 by 15.3% (0.153) and enter the result.*

> *(B) More than $55,500 but less than $130,200, multiply the amount in excess of $55,500 by 2.9% (0.029). Add $8,491.50 to the result and enter the total.*

> *(C) $130,200 or more, enter $10,657.80.*

Quite often, the No. 2 tax exceeds the No. 1 tax. The reason for this is obvious. As you can see in Figure 10.2, there are no subtraction offsets against it. The only way to reduce the SE tax on line 5 is to reduce your net profit(s) in lines 1 and 2. If you can reduce your combined net earnings on line 3 to less than $400, your SE tax is zero.

## The 92.35% Parity Factor

On line 4 in Figure 10.2, the instruction says—

*Multiply line 3 by 0.9235.*

Where does this figure (0.9235 = 92.35%) come from?

Mathematically, it is 100% minus 7.65% (100 - 7.65 = 92.35). The 7.65% is one-half of the 15.3% combined social security and medicare tax rates (12.4% + 2.9% = 15.3%) for 1992.

If the same worker were employed instead of self-employed (same earnings base), instead of paying 15.3% as his social tax, he would pay one-half or 7.65%. His employer would pay the other one half or 7.65%.

In 1990, Congress sought to more nearly equalize the social tax impact on both types of workers. It did so in two stages. One stage was to allow the "first multiplier" of the SE net earnings to be decreased by 7.65% [IRC Sec. 1402(a)(12)]. This is the line 4 multiplier 92.35% above. This is to provide employee parity.

The second stage provides for employer parity. An employer who pays the 7.65% social security/medicare tax for his employees gets a deduction against his No. 1 tax for full dollar amount of such tax. Prior to 1990, there was no corresponding deduction allowed for self-employeds. Upon enactment of Section 164(f): Deductible Taxes, self-employeds are now allowed a deduction against their total income on Form 1040, an amount equal to one-half of the dollar amount of line 5 of short Schedule SE.

At the very bottom of the short Schedule SE, there is a small print footnote which reads—

*Note: Also enter one-half of the amount from line 5 on **Form 1040, line** _____ [Adjustments to Income].*

Parity between employees, self-employeds, and employers, with respect to the No. 2 tax, may never be 100%. The principal reason for ongoing disparity is that employees-employers pay the No. 2 tax on gross earnings, whereas self-employeds pay it on net earnings.

## The "Long" Schedule SE

The long form Schedule SE is exactly what its name implies. It is a "long form." Whereas the short SE consists of five lines, the long SE consists of 30 lines. The first three lines of both forms are the same: the profits and losses from Schedules C, F, and K-1. From this point on, there are vast differences when using the long form.

The long form provides for an "optional method" for SE tax computation. This method enables low earnings self-employeds to make sufficient social security/medicare contributions that qualify them for the minimum earnings test for receiving social security benefits later. To use the optional method, gross farm income must not be more than $2,400 and nonfarm net earnings must not be less than $400.

Certain church employees are treated as self-employeds, which the long SE accommodates. Unreported tip income by certain employees also is accommodated on the long SE. So, too, is Tier 1 railroad retirement compensation.

By far the main thrust of the long form Schedule SE is the two preprinted lines which read (for 1992) as follows:

*Maximum amount of **combined** wages and self-employment earnings subject to social security tax* $55,500

*Maximum amount of **combined** wages and self-employment earnings subject to medicare tax* $130,200

The idea behind these two lines is to give priority tax credit to employment wages before computing the tax on self-employment earnings. The maximum base for the No. 2 tax is the same, whether one is employed, self-employed, or some combination of the two.

The bottom line on the long Schedule SE is the self-employment tax only. Any employee-employer tax has been segregated out by the computational procedures.

Actually, the short SE and long SE are on one and the same Schedule SE. The distinction is made simply by calling the short form Section A (page 1) and the long form Section B (page 2). Our contention is that once you become fully self-employed — as is the goal and thesis of this book — the Section B long form is of little ongoing interest to you.

## Mating With Form 1040

Schedule SE attaches directly to your personal income tax return, Form 1040. If you and your spouse are each required to prepare a Schedule SE, you need some quick way to distinguish them. As a suggestion, in the upper right-hand corner of each SE, mark, respectively, (H) for husband and (W) for wife. Both SE's attach to your joint return (if you file jointly).

No matter how many self-employed businesses each spouse may have, the bottom line tax on each Schedule SE is one amount. However, when there are two separate spousal amounts, they combine and enter on Form 1040 as one amount. To make the combined entry more self-explanatory, it is a good idea to insert to the left of the single columnar entry a breakdown such as: $_____ (H); $_____ (W). This is for tracing purposes should, several years later, one of the spousal SE's be changed . . . for whatever reason.

Whether the short or long Schedule SE is used, the instructions below the last line entry (self-employment tax) say—

*Enter here and on Form 1040, line  Y .*
*Also enter one-half of amount on Form 1040, line  X .*

The line X is designated on Form 1040, **page 1**, as—

*One-half of self-employment tax* _____

This line appears near the bottom of page 1 in the section labeled: *Adjustments to Income.*

There are other potential adjustments to income, such as retirement plan contributions, alimony payments, etc. When all such adjustments are totaled, they are subtracted from your total income on Form 1040 to arrive at your Adjusted Gross Income (AGI). It is from this AGI that your No. 1 tax (regular income tax) evolves.

The line Y above is designated on Form 1040, **page 2**, as—

*Self-employment tax (attach Schedule SE)* _____

This entry line appears about midway down page 2 in the section labeled: *Other Taxes.* There are other "other taxes" such as alternative minimum tax, recapture tax, tax on early withdrawal of retirement plans, etc. Of the other taxes, the SE tax is the first one officially listed. This is why we have consistently referred to the SE tax as the No. 2 tax. Commenting on the No. 3 tax, the No. 4 tax, etc. is beyond the scope of our discussion.

To depict the situation at this point, we present Figure 10.3. Note that 50% of SE tax goes on page 1 of Form 1040, where it is *subtracted* from your total income (business, nonbusiness, investment, other). In contrast, note that 100% of the SE tax goes on page 2, where it is *added* to the No. 1 tax (and to No. 3, etc., if any). Thus, when the total amount of tax indicated on your return is paid, the payment automatically includes the SE tax. No separate payment of this tax is required.

## Now, the ES Tax

Once you have prepared your Form 1040 return, and computed your total tax for the completed year, you have to immediately turn

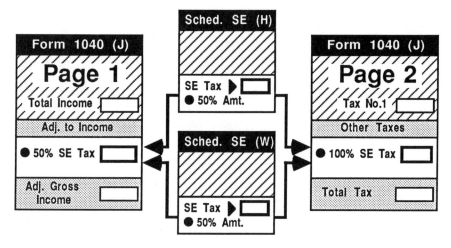

**Fig. 10.3 - The Mating of Schedule(s) SE with Form 1040 (J)**

your attention to the current year and *prepay* your tax thereon. This is the estimated (ES) tax mandate of Section 6654(a). In pertinent part, this mandate reads—

> *Every individual shall make a declaration of his estimated tax for the taxable year . . . except where—*
> *(1)   the tax is less than $500,* [or]
> *(2)   there was no liability for tax for the preceding taxable year of 12 months.* [Sec. 6654(e)(1), (2)]

In other words, you have to estimate in advance what your total tax (No. 1, No. 2, No. 3, etc.) is going to be and prepay it throughout the year.

Many self-employeds deeply resent this ES tax imposition as another irritant of Big Government. This resentment is understandable. Self-employeds face many income and expense uncertainties in the upcoming year. They have to contend with many pressures from governments (federal, state, local), customers, suppliers, creditors, workers, and others. This makes it very difficult to estimate what the upcoming year's total tax will be. But try to explain this to the IRS. If you do, it booms at you the *underpayment penalty* of Section 6621(a)(2).

On April 15th, you have to pay in full your previous calendar year's tax. You ALSO have to pay 25% of your ES tax for the current calendar year. The overall effect is that you pay 125% of your tax at that time.

ES taxpayers need only prepay 90% of the actual tax for the current year, or 100% of the tax for the preceding year . . . *whichever is lesser* [Sec. 6654(d)]. But even this little variance is snatched away if your income in the current year exceeds $40,000 of your previous year's income. The ES tax burden can become a nightmare if you are habitually cash short.

## ES Voucher Forms

Your ES tax prepayments are not sent to the IRS carte blanche. You have to fill out a special check-size tax form: *ES Payment-Voucher*. There are four such payment vouchers for the ES tax year: **1**, **2**, **3**, and **4**. Each is sequentially numbered in bold print corresponding to each sequential due date. On each voucher, you must enter your correct name and SSN, and that of your spouse (if any), and the dollar amount of the payment you are making. You must enclose your payment with the correct voucher number (1, 2, 3, or 4) for which the due date applies. All four ES payments have the preprinted due dates as follows:

    Voucher 1  —  April 15th
    Voucher 2  —  June 15th
    Voucher 3  —  September 15th
    Voucher 4  —  January 15th

The January payment is the 4th payment for the designated ES year. It is *not* the 1st payment for the upcoming ES year. This often causes confusion for ES recordkeeping. To minimize this confusion, all four payment vouchers are **bold dated** with the calendar year to which they apply.

For estimating your ES tax, the IRS furnishes — or will furnish upon request — its Form 1040-ES: *Estimated Tax for Individuals*. There are instructions with this form; there is a computational worksheet; there is a separate line for your SE (No. 2) tax; there are tax rate schedules for the No. 1 tax; there is a handy chart for keeping track of your payments; and there is a list of IRS addresses, one of which will be where you file your voucher with payment.

The 1040-ES instructions also post a clear warning: *When a Penalty is Applied*. The warning says—

*In some cases, you may owe a penalty when you file your ES return. The penalty is imposed on each underpayment for the number of days it remains unpaid. A penalty may be applied if you did not pay enough estimated tax, or you did not make the payments on time or in the required amount..*

The underpayment penalty averages about 0.03% per day of lateness, per dollar of underpayment. As tax penalties go, this is not severe. It is comparable to paying interest on borrowed money. Some self-employeds opt to pay the penalty rather than cash-starving their business. The penalty is intentionally set at 3% *above* the prime lending rate at commercial banks.

## Tips on ES Payments

We all have enough taxes to worry about, without fussing and fretting over those ES payments throughout the year. If you set your mind to it, and discipline yourself as you should, there is a practical way to put your affairs at ease. It hinges on getting your Form 1040 return done: **completed, filed, and paid** — by January 31st.

As per Code Section 6654(h), a special rule applies when your annual return is filed on or before January 31 of each year. This rule reads in full as follows:

*If, on or before January 31 of the following taxable year, the taxpayer files a return for the taxable year and pays in full the amount computed on the return as payable, then no addition to tax shall be imposed under subsection (a) with respect to any underpayment of the 4th required installment.*

Think about this for a moment. If you get your affairs in order and your regular return filed in January (instead of April 15th), there are only three ES vouchers to file. Don't use the excuse that you are waiting for some 1099's to come in. As a good recordkeeper, you should know at all times what your income is. If you are off significantly, you can always amend your return. So, get it filed by January 31st.

Doing so, gives you time between January 31 and April 15 to accumulate cash for your first ES payment: Voucher 1. Then, without all of the ES worksheet hassles, take the simple approach.

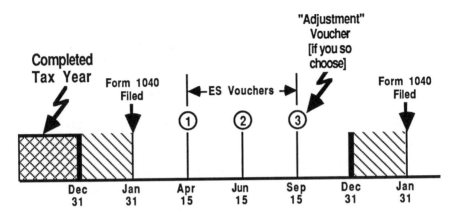

**Fig. 10.4 - The 3 ES Payment Cycle: January Start**

Use the total tax (No. 1, No. 2, No. 3, etc.) that you just paid for the completed year, as your projected estimate. Round it up or round it down, based on your "gut feeling" as to what you expect to do in the current year. Don't try to fine tune it. Use nice round numbers that, when divisible by 3, come out to even $100 or $1,000 amounts.

Make each of your 3-only payments one-third of your gut estimate for the year. If your actual income turns out to be less than your ES tax estimate, you'll get an overpayment credit, or you can choose not to make the 3rd payment. If your actual income increases dramatically, you can increase your 3rd payment proportionately, or pay the balance due by January 31st. The penalty, if any, will be minimal.

We depict this three-ES-payment program in Figure 10.4. Once you get the cycle set up, and you file your regular returns each January, you have more constructive time to attend to business. You are freed of that panic of always trying to catch up with tax-due deadlines.

# 11

# THE AUDIT STRIKE

---

**There Are Two Basic Types of IRS Audits: OFFICE And FIELD. Office Audits Last 1 To 2 Hours And Focus On Limited Specific Items. Field Audits Last 1 To 2 DAYS And Are Unlimited As To Business Expenditures And Bank Deposits. Selection Is By DIF-Scoring, For Maximum Additional Revenue — And Penalties — Pursuant To Section 7602(a). Completion Is Signified With A REPORT OF EXAMINATION CHANGES. Disagreement Requires A Capsulated Statement Of Disputed Issues, Facts, And Tax Law. Field Auditors Always "Find Something" Even If De Minimis, Insubstantial, And Unreasonable. As Per Section 7605(c), There Is No Protection Against Repetitive And Harassing Audits.**

---

Sooner or later, every fully self-employed individual will be tax audited. This goes with the territory. Expect it.

If your business gross receipts are less than $50,000, the audit probably will be later. If your gross receipts exceed $100,000, the audit probably will be sooner. If your gross receipts approach $1,000,000 you'll face repetitive audits every two to three years.

The biggest problem with an IRS audit is psychological. Small business owners dread and fear it. Those who do, most likely have kept poor records, or have had bad experience in responding to the IRS's many computer-matching inquiries. Whether you win, lose, or draw in an audit, the experience will make you a different citizen and a better business person. The earlier in your business career that you obtain this experience, the more you'll profit later.

Despite the IRS's hoopla, there is no such thing as a "routine" audit. Every audit is conducted for one purpose only. It is to take additional money out of your pocket. It is not to educate you, or to commend you for the taxes you pay. It is a *money enforcement tool*. In the process, your "spreading the word" will intimidate others and soften them into forking over more of their hard-earned money voluntarily to government. Thus, you should treat every audit as an opportunity to learn more about our tax system, and to develop ways to use the system more to your advantage.

In this chapter, therefore, we want to tell you about the two principal types of audits (office and field), the selection process, the preliminary questioning that goes on (that borders on invading your financial privacy), and the role of your bank accounts. As a self-employed, it is always your bank records that the IRS is after. And, of course, we want to give you some pointers on how to conduct yourself during an audit, and what to do before and afterwards.

## Authority to Examine

The IRS has extensive authority to examine any information that goes on a tax return, or that should have gone on it. This authority roots in Section 7602 of the Internal Revenue Code. Section 7602 is titled: *Examination of Books and Witnesses*. The term "books," here, means pertinent tax and financial records; the term "witnesses" means the taxpayer, his spouse, and other persons knowledgeable of the taxpayer's activities.

Section 7602 is embodied in Chapter 78 of the tax code, which is titled: *Discovery of Liability and Enforcement*. This title alone makes it quite clear that the objective of any audit examination is to "discover" additional tax liability and enforce its collection. It is the degree of the IRS's aggressiveness and obsessiveness with discovery that worries most taxpayers. Where do you draw the line between abuse of power, disregard of rights, and reasonable compliance with law? The IR Code does not say.

Section 7602(a): *Authority to Summons, Etc.*, says in pertinent part that—

*For the purpose of ascertaining the correctness of any return, making a return where none has been made, determining the liability of any person for any internal revenue tax . . ., or collecting any such liability, the [IRS] is authorized—*

*(1) To examine any books, papers, records, or other data which may be relevant or material to such inquiry;*

*(2) To summon the person liable for tax or required to perform the act, . . . to appear before the [IRS] at a time and place named in the summons and to produce such books, papers, records, or other data, and to give such testimony, under oath, as may be relevant or material to such inquiry; and*

*(3) To take such testimony of the person concerned, under oath, as may be relevant or material to such inquiry.*

The only statutory limitation to the IRS's authority is the phrase: *may be relevant or material to such inquiry.* This phrase is repeated in each of paragraphs (1), (2), and (3) above.

Who judges that which "may be relevant," etc.? These are matters which are left entirely up to the examining agent — and to his or her pet peeves and whims. Most such agents, at least initially, try to be reasonable. But their sense of reasonableness and that of the summoned taxpayer often differ dramatically. If you'll reread Section 7602(a) above, you'll find no sense of toning down the IRS's awesome power of examination unlimited.

The IRS's audit power is extended in Regulation 301.7602-1(a), (b). The disturbing phrases therein are—

*(a) For . . . determining the liability of any person for any internal revenue tax (including any interest, additional amount, addition to the tax, or civil penalty) or . . .*

*(b) This summons power may be used in an investigation of either civil or criminal tax-related liability. [Emphasis added.]*

The whole idea of this regulation is to maximize tax revenue under any pretext.

## The Selection Process

Self-employed individuals tend to be audited more frequently than fully employed persons and large businesses. This is probably because small-business entrepreneurs tend to be risk takers. The IRS interprets this characteristic as risk-taking with the tax laws. So, it sets its sights accordingly.

Of all returns selected for audit, about 95% are selected through a mathematical process called *DIF-Scoring.* The "DIF" means:

Discriminate Information Function. This is a statistical sampling process using secret probability formulas at the IRS's National Computer Center in Martinsburg, West Virginia. The other 5% of audit selections are based on "red flagging" by IRS classifiers, agents, and investigators either at the regional processing centers or at local district offices.

All tax returns go through a regional processing center where they are examined for general acceptability. This is called "acceptance screening." The returns are examined for proper signatures, all required attachments, arithmetic correctness, and whether any unusual items or attachments appear. A Document Locator Number (DLN) is assigned to each return, and a summary tape is prepared. All summaries are electronically punched into master tapes and sent to the National Computer Center. There all returns are DIF-scored. See Figure 11.1 for a general overview of the selection process.

We make no pretense of knowing what the official DIF-scoring range is. For the sake of instructional purposes only, let us *assume* that the scores range from 1 to 699. If so, those returns scoring from 1 to 99 would be audit safe. Those scoring from 600 to 699 would be audit guaranteed. Scores of 300 and above would be *high-DIF* returns. These are the returns for which there is a high probability of collecting additional revenue — and penalties — from taxpayers.

The final selection is done at an IRS District Office near where the taxpayer resides. A staff member (Returns Program Management) reviews each high-DIF return and assesses its potential for producing additional revenue. On those returns he selects, he marks particular items that he wants the auditor to scrutinize. Auditors need not limit their examinations to the particular marked items, but they must at least address them. The staff member also estimates the approximate amount of time that an auditor must spend on each selected return.

## Two Basic Audit Types

For overall revenue enforcement, many types of audits are performed. There are those canvassing (research) audits that we discussed in Chapter 8: Surveillance Matters. There also are training audits (to train IRS personnel), protester audits (of persons classed as tax protesters), TCMP audits (Total Compliance Measurement Program), collection enforcement audits (for

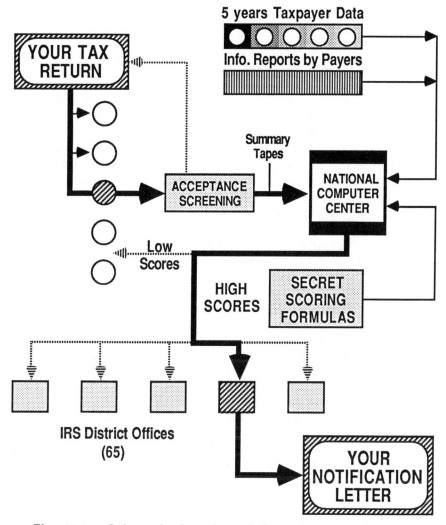

**5 years Taxpayer Data**

**Info. Reports by Payers**

**YOUR TAX RETURN**

**ACCEPTANCE SCREENING**

Summary Tapes

**NATIONAL COMPUTER CENTER**

Low Scores

**HIGH SCORES**

**SECRET SCORING FORMULAS**

**IRS District Offices (65)**

**YOUR NOTIFICATION LETTER**

**Fig. 11.1 - Schematic Overview of Audit Selection Process**

determining location of assets), prime-issue audits, correspondence audits, civil audits for fraud, criminal audits for tax evasion, investigating audits (in conjunction with other government agencies), and so on. For the most part, these audits constitute the 5% non-DIF returns.

By far, 95% of those returns selected for audit have been DIF-scored as having "high probability" for additional revenue. For these returns, two basic types of audit procedures are used. One procedure is called the *office audit*; the other is the *field audit*. The two differ substantially in the amount of audit time and intensity by the IRS.

Office audits are classed as such because the auditee is summoned into the IRS District Office nearest his personal residence. He is directed to bring with him specific records, for a specific year or years. An office audit lasts from one to two hours usually: three hours at most. This time is exclusive of any additional records or information that the auditor may request.

Office auditors are case-volume oriented. They have to perform several audits a day. Their "performance quota" — the amount of additional revenue they are expected to produce — is estimated at between $200 and $300 per hour of audit time. These auditors are paid a salary of between $20,000 and $30,000 per year, depending on entry experience and seniority.

In contrast, field audits are conducted at the taxpayer's residence or place of business, or at some other location that is not an IRS office. Field audits are more time-consuming and more complex. They are depth-oriented and tend to include most all business entries (income and expenses) on a selectee's return. To properly "do their thing," field auditors must be provided with adequate desk or table space by the taxpayer. Field audits last at least one full day (eight hours), though in most cases, two full audit days are involved. In special cases, the on-site audit may last as long as three days.

Field auditors are more experienced than office auditors. Their salaries range from $30,000 to $40,000 per year depending on title and tenure. Field auditors tend to be very picky, stuffy, and arrogant. They are under strict orders to "find something" on every auditee. This leads them to threaten and intimidate auditees. Their performance quota is estimated at between $300 and $500 of additional revenue per hour of audit time.

As per Regulation 301.7605-1T(d)(3)(ii), (iii), the IRS will agree not to conduct a field examination at the taxpayer's place of business—

*If the business is so small that doing so would essentially require the taxpayer to close the business or would unduly disrupt business operations.*

As a self-employed business owner, having an IRS agent parked at a desk or table for one to three days at your place of business is indeed disruptive. It is disruptive to you, to your clients, to your customers, to your suppliers, and to your workers. If you claim disruption, you must provide a satisfactory alternate place — with all of your books, records, and source documents — for the auditor to work.

Even if you provide an alternate site, you must allow the auditor to visit your place of business or residence. The reason for this, the regulation above says, is—

*To establish facts that can only be established by direct visit, such as inventory or asset verification . . . on a normal work day . . . during normal business hours.*

## Notification Letters

Except for undercover audits and criminal investigations, IRS auditors don't suddenly appear at your door demanding to see your books, records, and documents. For office audits, you are sent a written notification. For field audits, the auditor phones in advance, then follows up with a written notification. Each notification letter is an official summons. You are given very little choice in matters other than date, time, and place.

An audit notification letter has no salutation of any kind. There is no "Dear Taxpayer"; no "Dear Auditee"; no "Dear Selectee"; or any other humanized greeting. There is no functional title or other quick-identifying heading. The notice comes in a brown, window-type envelope with the sender's name: **Internal Revenue Service**, bold-printed thereon. When you open it, the very first sentence reads—

*Your Federal income tax return has been selected for examination.*

Presumably, it is this succinctness that gets your immediate attention. Then, after you de-spin your brain, you read on—

*On the reverse side please see the specific items to be examined for the tax year(s) shown below. It is very important that you contact our office within 10 days from the date of this letter. . . .*

*Without the requested documents, we will have to proceed on the basis of information available.*

The sentence about "basis of information available" is a warning to you. If you don't show up, or if you show up but don't provide the documents requested, all specific items listed on the reverse side (or at the end of the letter) will be disallowed in full. Thereupon, you will be billed and penalized . . . also in full. This is called a *default audit*. Such can be very costly.

A field audit notification letter is more terse than that above. Otherwise, the first page of the letter is similar to that for an office audit. The main difference is that the field audit notice has no reverse side. In its place, there is enclosed an ominous-looking form: *Information Document Request* (Form 4564). This request lists everything that the auditor can think of. Since a field auditor is assigned 1, 2, or 3 days to examine your return, he/she wants to make sure that you provide enough documents to justify the amount of audit time assigned.

An actual example of a field audit document request is given in Figure 11.2. Please glance over it carefully. It's quite allsweeping. Could **you** stand this kind of audit heat?

## The Initial Probing

When you get an audit notification letter, make sure that the date, time, and place are satisfactory to you. Don't disrupt your activities to be overly accommodating to the auditor. He/she is on the government payroll; there is no incentive to perform efficiently or promptly. Other than being humane and courteous, don't go out of your way to try to please. But don't be confrontational. All auditors have a legitimate job to do.

In the preliminary phase of an audit, you will be asked many probing questions. This is because each auditor has an official worksheet outline which he or she must follow. The outline is Form 4700: *Examination Workpapers*. There are two supplemental worksheets, namely: A — General and B — Business. Most of the questions on these probe-sheet outlines are check-off boxes with blank spaces for handwritten notes and comments. These are the IRS's internal workpapers and are not subject to your review. However, you'll get a computer printout of the auditor's "findings" later.

Probesheet A (General) addresses such matters as—

| Form 4564 | INFORMATION DOCUMENT REQUEST | Date of Request |
|---|---|---|

**TO:** Name of Taxpayer: _____ RNF _____   Subject: _____ Sched. C _____

Name of Business: _____ JLS _____   SSN or EIN: _____

## Description of Documents Requested

1. All income Forms W-2, 1099, and K-1.
2. Bank statements, cancelled checks, and deposit slips for all bank accounts: business AND personal.
3. All savings accounts (passbooks, CD's, T-Bills, etc.).
4. All investment accounts (mutual funds, brokerage firms, private parties).
5. Records of any nontaxable income received (loans, gifts, inheritances, insurance, sales, etc.).
6. All workpapers used to prepare and reconcile your return.
7. Verification of Schedule C Gross Receipts.
8. Verification of Schedule C Cost of Goods Sold.
9. Invoices on all depreciable assets acquired during year.
10. Verification of the following Schedule C expenses:

   a. Advertising
   b. Car & truck
   c. Freight & postage
   d. Legal & professional
   e. Insurance     For Tax Year
   f. Rent          **1991**
   g. Repairs
   h. Supplies
   i. Office expense
   j. Travel

ALSO, PRIOR AND SUBSEQUENT TAX RETURNS ( _____ 1990 _____ and _____ 1992 _____ ).

**FROM:** Name and Title of Requester _____ JJH, REVENUE AGENT _____

IRS office and Phone No. _____

**Information Due By:**

☐ Appointment

☐ Mail In

Fig. 11.2 - Example of Requested Documents for Field Audit

1. Prior IRS contacts and prior audits, if any.
2. All due returns filed; any amended returns.

3. Income probe: sales of assets, hobbies, investments, gambling winnings, prizes and awards, loans, gifts, inheritances, etc.
4. Bartering probe: services, merchandise, trades.
5. Foreign accounts and trusts.

Probesheet B (Business) addresses such matters as—

1. Day-to-day business operations and history.
2. Accounting method: how/where books kept.
3. Gross receipts: cash, check, other; how recorded.
4. Cash on hand; home, business, elsewhere.
5. Bank accounts and banking practices.
6. Location of business assets; any safe boxes.
7. Loans, notes, mortgages outstanding.
8. Accounts receivable: returns and allowances.
9. Capital items purchased or sold.
10. Related transactions: business and family.

Answer any of these questions that are pertinent, in a straight-forward manner. Avoid giving details. You may bristle at some of the questions: your government — your IRS — can get awfully nosey. Try to slough off the irrelevant and immaterial as tactfully as you can. The auditor is just probing. He/she is trying to get a sense of your weakesses that might lead to additional revenue.

## Examination Procedure: General

Whether an office or field audit is involved, the probing questions above will be asked. At the conclusion of the probing, the auditor poses the opportunity question. He/she asks—

"Is there anything else that you want to tell me about at this time?"

. . . or words to this effect.

This is your opportunity to point out any errors or oversights on your part. In the six to 18 months following the filing of a return, some items — such as omitted income, overlooked deductions, errors in arithmetic — may come out of the woodwork. If they directly affect the return(s) being audited, disclose them. Get them out on the table. By doing so, you free your mind to stand toe-to-

toe with the auditor when he/she examines specific items on your return(s).

Office auditors, bless their souls, stick closely to the specific items check-boxed on the reverse side or at the end of your notification letter. So, you bring to the audit only what is asked for. When you are asked for item A, for example, find it in your records and hand it to the auditor. When asked for item B, give item B. The same for item C, and so on. Give nothing or say nothing that is not asked for. An office audit is not a confessional. Stick to the issues officially raised, and DON'T RAISE OTHER ISSUES on your own. Office auditors will generally tell you as they go along whether an item is O.K., not O.K., or not fully substantiated as claimed on your return. They are reasonably communicative person-to-person.

Field auditors, damn their hides, are aloof and snippy. They'll have you identify all the Figure 11.2 documents that you've laid out for them. Other than letting you explain what the records are, and how they interface with other records, they won't discuss any examination items with you. They ask that you excuse yourself and leave them alone. They'll call you back when they need you.

Because field auditors are assigned a certain number of days to work on your return(s), they have to spend the time, whether you are well prepared or not. If you are well prepared, they doodle and dawdle. Naturally, they don't want you around when they do so. They make copious notes to satisfy their supervisors that the 8, 12, 16, 24, or more hours assigned were well spent.

In an office audit, one in five audits (approximately) results in *No Change*. A "no change" audit means that no additional tax revenue results. Office auditing staffs make up for the no changes by virtue of the volume of audits they perform.

In contrast, in a field audit, one in 15 to 20 audits results in no change. It's an ego and professionalism thing with these auditors. They spend so much time on an audit — 8 to 16 hours typically — that they just HAVE TO COME UP WITH SOMETHING.

## Bank Deposits Analysis

One area that field auditors love to wade into is your bank deposits and financial transactions. They do this to reconstruct your business income and compare it with the gross receipts that you report on Schedule C (Form 1040). The procedure they use for this is called: *bank deposits analysis*. The idea is that all of your deposits into all of your accounts are treated as tax-reportable income, unless you can establish otherwise.

Establishing "otherwise" is a formidable task. Particularly so if you have multiple accounts and you switch money back and forth frequently. If you engage in electronic transfers, revolving credit lines, direct deposits by computer, and sporadic deposits by mail or in person, your depository trails get pretty blurred by the end of the year. You become hopelessly lost and unable to explain each deposit explicitly. When you start to fumble and give inconsistent explanations, the auditor know he/she has you on the run.

In Figure 11.2, the auditor asked Schedule C taxpayer RNF (her true initials) for **all** of her monthly bank statements: business AND personal. He also asked for **all** savings accounts, **all** investment accounts, and **all** nontaxable income accounts. The auditee was a language translator who had bank accounts in Germany and Japan as well as the United States. Altogether, she had six separate accounts. She laid them all out in an orderly manner. She, with the help of her accountant, marked all deposits which were transfers, loans, paper reportings, and nontaxables. Then she let the auditor go to work "analyzing" them on his own.

The reconstruction/verification of income by bank deposits analysis goes like this—

Step 1 — Add all deposits (for the audit year) for each account separately.

Step 2 — Grand total the deposits for all accounts.

Step 3 — Add all transfers between accounts and subtract from Step 2.

Step 4 — Add all loan and credit-line deposits and subtract from Step 2.

Step 5 — Add all payer reportings (Forms 1099) that show up elsewhere on the return (other than on Schedule C) and subtract from Step 2.

Step 6 — Add all nontaxable deposits, such as gifts, inheritances, federal tax refunds, insurance proceeds, tax exempt interest, etc., and subtract form Step 2.

Step 7 — Compare the adjusted gross deposits in Step 6 with gross receipts reported on Schedule C.
— If the discrepancy is de minimis, accept the gross receipts as reported.
— If the discrepancy is substantial, **add** the deposit difference to gross receipts.

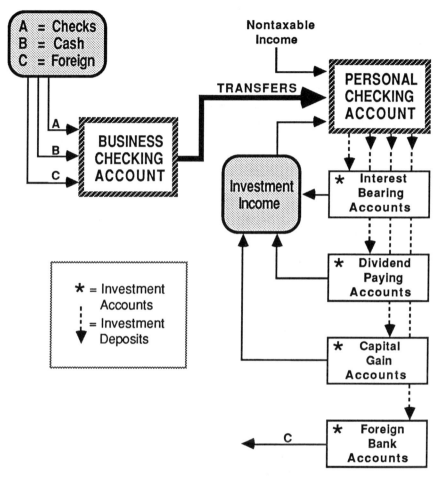

**Fig. 11.3 - Disciplined Bank Deposits Accounting of Income**

In the particular auditee's case of Figure 11.2, the adjusted gross deposits were $1,261,718. The discrepancy between this amount and the gross receipts reported on her Schedule C was a mere $526. How did she do it? She was a well disciplined bank depositor.

There is a secret to surviving a bank deposits analysis. That secret is: Have TWO (only) basic depository accounts: one business, one personal. Have all **initial** deposits (business into business; personal into personal) go into only these accounts. Then transfer money from these two accounts into as many other accounts as you want.  Make the transfers in even $1,000 amounts so that they are clearly traceable.  We've tried to portray this secret in Figure 11.3.  Please take a moment to study this figure.

## Report of Audit Changes

When an auditor completes his/her examination of your return, he reviews his various workpapers and makes certain adjustment determinations.  These adjustments — called: *examination changes* — are mailed to you as a "report."  This report is highly computerized, stodgy, stereotyped, and devoid of any helpful explanations.  It is accompanied by a cover letter which makes certain demands upon you.  Typically, a change report comes in the mail to you between 30 and 60 days after completion of the audit.

Depending on the procedures at the IRS District Office which sent you the audit notification letter, the *Report of Income Tax Examination Changes* may run anywhere from five to 15 pages of computer printout sheets.  Whether an office audit or a field audit, all reports start with—

*Adjustments to Income and/or Deductions*

This starting point is followed by various statement entries which we summarize in Figure 11.4.

The cover letter to the report states the time within which you must respond.  This is usually 30 days.  Within this time you must either—

(a) Agree in full with the report,
(b) Agree in part/disagree in part, or
(c) Disagree in full.

If you agree in full, you must sign an agreement form, waive all of your rights to appeal, and pay the additional tax, penalty, and interest which has accrued since the due date of the return.

If you disagree in part or in full, you should request a conference with the Regional Office of Appeals.  If the change report is for $2,500 or less (including penalties), you may signify your intention to appeal by telephone.  If the change report is for $10,000 or less, you must signify your intention in a brief written statement of the disputed issues.  If the change report is for more

| Report of Income Tax EXAMINATION CHANGES | | Dept. of the Treasury Internal Revenue Service | |
|---|---|---|---|
| Name & Address of Taxpayer | | SSN or EIN | |
| | | Form | Year(s) |
| Adjustments to Income &/or Deductions | | Year(s) Ending | |
| | | 1990 | 1991 | 1992 |
| 1. Adjustments | | | | |
| (a) (d) | | | | |
| (b) (e) | | | | |
| (c) (f) | | | | |
| 2. Total adjustments | | | | |
| 3. Taxable Income per return | | | | |
| 4. Corrected taxable income | | | | |
| 5. Correct tax liability [No.1] | | | | |
| 6. Less credits | | | | |
| 7. Balance after credits | | | | |
| 8. Other taxes [No.2, etc.] | | | | |
| 9. Total corrected tax liability | | | | |
| 10. Total tax shown on return | | | | |
| 11. DEFICIENCY | | | | |
| 12. PENALTIES | | | | |
| (a) | | | | |
| (b) | | | | |
| (c) | | | | |
| 13. INTEREST | | | | |
| 14. TOTAL AMOUNT DUE ▶ | | | | |
| Examiner's Name | | IRS District | Date |

Fig. 11.4 - Summary of Information and Audit Change Report

than $10,000, you must file a formal written protest. The written protest must state succinctly—

1. The unagreed adjustments
   — by item and amount
2. The reason for disagreement
   — by item and reason
3  The tax law on which you rely
   — IRC section and/or specific regulation

## When-to-Disagree Example

If you have a plausible basis for disagreeing with an auditor's change report, you should do so. To illustrate what we think is a plausible basis, we cite the following real-life example. This is taxpayer RNF whom we identified in Figure 11.2. We are citing RNF's case because it verifies that a self-employed individual can indeed generate in excess of $1,000,000 in gross receipts.

The auditee (a woman) had a Schedule C language translation business, comprised of nine employees and 68 nonemployees. Her gross receipts reported for the audit year totaled $1,262,244. The discrepancy with her adjusted bank deposits was $526. That is, she reported $526 *more* than the auditor's analysis of her bank deposits revealed. Her cost of goods sold was $662,647 which was substantiated to the penny. Her total operating expenses came to $256,899. These, too, were substantiated to the penny. She acquired a 25-year-old commercial building that year which cost her $565,000 including land. She also acquired $27,119 in computers and accessories. Her prior depreciable assets, excluding vehicles, totaled $175,057 . . . all of which were verified.

So, what did the auditor find wrong?

Nothing, really. But, being a field auditor spending 16 hours on a return, he had to find something. The classic "gotta-find-something" procedure is to recharacterize (that is, reclassify) selected expenditures as capital items. This is exactly what the auditor did.

He reclassified the following expenditures by capitalizing them. These were:

(a) Office furniture: $1,636
  — among existing depreciable assets of $175,057
  "Error" = 0.93%

(b) Building repairs: $3,924
  — to a $350,000 building depreciated over 31.5 years
  "Error" = 1.12%

(c) Floor covering: $5,458
  — to a $350,000 building depreciated over 31.5 years
  "Error" = 1.56%

(d) Computer parts: $7,149
  — out of expenditures for the year totaling $256,899
  "Error" = 2.78%

For these recharacterizations, the auditee was assessed an additional tax of $5,589. The amount of tax (No. 1 and No. 2) that she had already paid was $62,750. Nevertheless, by his recharacterization to "find something," the auditor met his performance quota of $350 per hour ($5,589 ÷ 16 hrs = $349.13/hr).

## How to Disagree

We don't know how you interpret the auditor's performance above. We think it's another manifestation of the nit-picking that often characterizes the IRS. The "gotta-find-something" behavior only generates disrespect for that agency. Unfortunately, you cannot convey this disrespect in your statement of disagreement. Nor can you apply any de minimis exception based on reasonableness and common sense. You have to stick to the issues, facts, and (tax) law. Let us explain.

If you want to disagree with the IRS, you have to prepare a STATEMENT OF DISPUTED ISSUES. You state that you disagree with the auditor's findings and that you request a conference with an appeals officer. Then you list the unagreed issues with your corresponding reasons for disagreement. Capsulate your reasons: you'll get a chance to expand on them later.

For example, in the above matter of the $1,636 office furniture recharacterization, you might object because—

Replacing $1,636 of office chairs among existing depreciable equipment amounting to $175,057 is "de minimis, insubstantial, and does not significantly disproportionate the allocation of costs." **Temp. Reg. 1-263A-1T(b)(3)(iii)(A)(2).**

In the case of repairs for $3,924 recharacterized as building improvements, you might object because—

Plumbing and electrical repairs in the amount of $3,924 to a $350,000 commercial building constitutes "incidental repairs and maintenance: not capital expenditures." **Reg. 1-263(a)-1(b).**

In the case of computer parts for $7,149, you might object because—

Miscellaneous computer parts, extension plugs, and limited-use software (in the amount of $7,149) separately and irregularly purchased in conjunction with $27,119 in computers and accessories (which were depreciated) plus other materials and supplies amounting to $79,195 (on 65 separate invoices), truly constitutes "supplies and small tools" in total verified Schedule C expenditures amounting to $256,899. **Reg. 1.162-3.**

The instructions in the audit change cover letter tell you to return a copy of the cover letter with your Statement of Disputed Issues. These instructions also warn you that, pursuant to IRS Section 6673—

*The tax court can impose a penalty of up to $25,000 . . . if the court finds that* [you] *instituted the proceedings primarily for delay,* [or if your] *position is found to be frivolous or groundless.*

This is the trouble with the IRS. Whenever you disagree, it floats a penalty past you as a subtle intimidation to keep you from disagreeing. If this tactic turns you into a wimp, then pay the additional tax and sign the agreement form.

## The 20% Accuracy Penalty

We're not through with taxpayer RNF yet. There's more.
The auditor was so confident that he had found something of substance against the taxpayer that he **added** the 20% accuracy penalty. That is, in his audit change report, he tacked on another $1,118 (20% x $5,589 = $1,118). Correspondingly, he entered the notation that—

*Since a portion of the underpayment of tax required to be shown on the return is attributable to one or more of (1) negligence or disregard of rules or regulations, (2) any substantial understatement of income tax, or (3) any substantial valuation overstatement, an addition to tax is charged as provided by Section 6662(a) of the Internal Revenue Code.*

How does this grab you?
From this computer wording, you can't tell what, specifically, the penalty is being assessed for. What is the auditor getting at —

other than increasing his performance quota by another $70 per hour ($1,118 penalty + 16 audit hours = $69.87/hr)?

Section 6662(c) defines "negligence" as—

*Any failure to make a reasonable attempt to comply with the* [tax code].

and defines "disregard" as—

*Any careless, reckless, or intentional disregard* [of the tax code].

Did the Schedule C taxpayer above demonstrate any negligence or carelessness? Is this why the 20% penalty is assessed? You be the judge. She had perfect records.

What about substantial understatement of tax? Or, substantial valuation overstatement? No valuation issue was raised by the auditor. So, the penalty has to be for substantial understatement.

On this point, Section 6662(d)(1)(A) says—

*There is a substantial understatement of income tax . . . if the amount of the understatement . . . **exceeds the greater of**—*
*(i)    10% of the tax required to be shown on the return, or*
*(ii)   $5,000.*                                            [Emphasis added.]

Hmm; this could be it. The required tax, according to the auditor, was $68,339. The tax actually shown on the return was $62,750. The difference is $5,589 — just over the line.

But Section 6662(d)(2)(B) says that—

*The amount of overstatement . . . **shall be reduced by** that portion of the understatement which is attributable to—*
*(i) the tax treatment of any item  by the taxpayer if there is or was substantial authority for such treatment.*
                                                            [Emphasis added.]

So, if RNF (above) quotes from a particular tax regulation that supports her position on the return, doesn't this justify reducing or eliminating the penalty? Why don't auditors themselves read the tax regulations?

The real truth is that most IRS auditors are lazy. It is so easy for them to assert a penalty because they know that **you** have to prove that *they* are wrong. This is the premise (presumption of correctness of the IRS) on which our entire tax system is based.

## Reasonable Cause Exception

Section 6664(c) says very clearly that—

*No penalty shall be imposed under this part* [addition to tax and assessable penalties] *with respect to any portion of an underpayment if it is shown that there was a reasonable cause for such portion and that the taxpayer acted in good faith with respect to such portion.* [Emphasis added.]

Establishing reasonable cause and showing good faith require a determined effort on your part to prove the IRS wrong. There is no exception to the 20% accuracy penalty unless you show convincing proof that the penalty should not apply.

Some guidance for meeting the reasonable cause exception to the accuracy penalty can be found in Regulation 1.6664-4(b)(1): *Facts and Circumstances Taken into Account.* The first two sentences of this regulation read—

*The determination of whether a taxpayer acted with reasonable cause and in good faith is made on a case-by-case basis, taking into account all pertinent facts and circumstances. The most important factor is the extent of the taxpayer's effort to assess* [his own] *proper tax liability . . . in attempting to file an accurate return.*

In RNF's case above, wasn't it a showing of good faith to submit to 16 hours of intensive examination of her Schedule C? The auditor found not $1 of omitted income from her $1,262,244 of gross receipts. Although he recharacterized and reclassified some items — which were purely his judgment call — she substantiated every penny of the $919,546 in cost of goods sold and operating expenses. How perfect do you have to be to please some auditors?

Needless to say, the taxpayer above protested the $1,118 accuracy penalty. In her capsule reason for disagreement, she wrote—

IRC 6664(c) provides a reasonable cause exception to the accuracy penalty where taxpayer acts in good faith. Taxpayer kept excellent records and **all**

**amounts** on Schedule C were audit verified precisely. The issue is one of recharacterization: a judgment call; it is **not** accuracy-related. **Reg. 1.6664-4(b)(1)**

What was the outcome of RNF's appeal from the auditor's change report?

For one, the 20% accuracy penalty was rescinded. In addition, the office chairs and computer parts were accepted as expense items, as originally posted. The electrical repairs and floor covering were capitalized (depreciated) over seven years (instead of over 31.5 years as the auditor wanted).

## Repetitive Audits

We have still one more item to tell you about concerning taxpayer RNF above. In a 7-year period, she's been audited three times! This is an audit every two to three years. This is repetitive; it borders on government harassment. This *is permissible* under the IR Code.

Section 7605(c): Restrictions on Examination of Taxpayer, on the surface, seems to address the matter of repetitive audits. This single-sentence statute says—

*No taxpayer shall be subjected to unnecessary examination or investigations, and only one inspection of a taxpayer's books of accounts shall be made for each taxable year unless the taxpayer requests otherwise or unless the [IRS], after investigation, notifies the taxpayer in writing that an additional inspection is necessary.*

What this means is that a taxpayer can be audited as often as the IRS wants. There is no regulatory clarification of what is meant by *unnecessary examination or investigations.* Consequently, the field examination division of the IRS can audit a self-employed taxpayer every consecutive year. And, because there are tons of tax laws, any examiner can "find something" to assess any time. Tragically, the Congress, the President, and the courts have turned deaf ears to taxpayer complaints of audit harassment.

As to **office audits only**, the IRS has a two-year no repetitive policy. When an office audit notification letter is sent out, it contains a paragraph which reads—

*To avoid any unnecessary repetitive examinations, let the appointment clerk know as soon as possible if your income tax return was examined for the same items listed at the end of this letter and the examination resulted in no change to your tax liability in either of the two prior years.*

Even this is waffling. The no-repetitive policy applies only if exactly the same items as before are being audited again, and the prior audit resulted in no change. As we said earlier, about one in five office audits result in no change. Thus, there is at least some chance of avoiding repetitive office audits.

As to field audits, however, no change is a rarity. This is because field auditors are under orders to "find something," no matter how small or how unreasonable it may be. Consequently, repetitive field audits "go with the territory" of successful small businesses. In actuality, field audits don't happen to Schedule C filers every consecutive year. But you should be prepared for such, nevertheless.

# 12

# KEOGH AND SEP PLANS

After 3 Years In Business, Adopting A Keogh Or SEP Plan For Retirement Purposes Makes Sense. It's Best To Use Those Master Prototype Plans Sponsored By Financial Institutions, And Approved By IRS As QUALIFIED TRUSTS Under Section 401(a). Contributions On Your Own Behalf Are Deductible On Form 1040; Contributions On Behalf Of Your Employees Are Deductible On Schedule C. "Defined" Contributions For Employees Maximize At 25% Of Compensation For Keoghs And At 15% For SEPs [20% And 13% Respectively, For Employers]. Special "Enhancement Opportunities" Exist For Self-Employeds Between Ages 59-1/2 And 70-1/2.

Self-employeds have one particular deduction on Form 1040 that their counterpart employeds do not have. This is an "off-the-top" deduction for contributions to qualified retirement plans, known as Keoghs and SEPs.

Contributions to these plans are deductible against the total income (business, nonbusiness, etc.) on page 1 of your Form 1040. The contributions are classed as an *adjustment* to income. When added to other adjustments (such as the 50% SE tax) and deducted from total income, you arrive at your adjusted gross income (AGI) for the taxable year. Your No. 1 tax derives from this AGI. Hence, a Keogh or SEP contribution can reduce your regular income tax for the contributory year.

The term "Keogh" (after its Congressional sponsor) came into being in 1974. It is used to distinguish between self-employed retirement plans, corporate retirement plans, and individual retirement accounts (IRAs). The term is still used today to denote this distinction, even though self-employment retirement plans and corporate plans are nearly on a par with each other. Whether self-employed or an employee of your own corporation, you can set up two or more Keogh plans.

The term SEP is the acronym for: Simplified Employee Pension. It is a single plan which is more simplified than having two or more plans under Keogh rules.

In this chapter, we want to discuss the distinctions between Keogh and SEP plans, and to point out the pros and cons of each. In both types of plans, where employees are involved, they, too, must be covered.

For the owners of self-employed businesses, contributions to Keogh and SEP plans can only be made if there is a net profit from the business. When there is a net loss, no deductible contributions can be made. This means that, when first starting your business, you may want to wait a few years to make sure that it is ongoing and profitable. We suggest waiting three years before getting Keogh/SEP involved. The reason for this 3-year wait period will become more apparent as you read on.

### Employee Excludability Limited

Aside from the need for a steady flow of cash for plan contributions, the most important decision-making factor concerning Keogh and SEP plans is the role of employees. Except for a very limited period of time, you cannot exclude employees. Whether you have one employee or 100 employees, you have to include them all, if each one meets certain conditions.

Foremost is the age and service condition. Specifically, an employee who is otherwise eligible MUST become a participant when he/she—

(1) attains age 21, and

For Keoghs—
(2) completes 1 year of service (variable vesting)
(3) completes 2 years of service (100% vesting)

For SEPs—
(4)    completes 3 years of service (100% vesting)

The term "year of service" means — for Keoghs — that an employee has worked not less than 1,000 hours in a 12-month period. For SEPs, a year of service is the working for at least one hour in any three out of five years.

The term "vesting" is an employee's nonforfeitable right to all or part of your contribution to his plan, after the statutory vesting period has been met. Only a Keogh plan allows variable vesting at 20% per year after completing one full year of service.

The rights to vesting bring up peripheral issues of discriminatory terminations, breaks in service, minimum funding, separate plan accounting for each employee, flexible versus inflexible plans (profit-sharing versus pension), and so on. There are literally tons of regulations on these matters. All target the disqualification of your Keogh or SEP plan if you trip over the discriminatory line.

Under the right conditions, the maximum contribution to either a Keogh or a SEP plan is $30,000 per year. The contributions are intended for the long haul. They are for retirement purposes and **not** for investment speculation.

Therefore, before you decide on a Keogh or SEP plan, you should give deep thought to what your employee/nonemployee situation is likely to be — 5, 10, 20 years or so away. The money you contribute to your employee participants is a Schedule C business expense deduction. However, the arithmetic is such that whatever you contribute to employees reduces the amount of contribution to your own Keogh or SEP plan.

## Compare Master Plans

Contributions to retirement plans of all types is big business for financial institutions. Because of the tax rules, contributions stay in each plan trust account 5, 10, 20 or more years. And each year, new contributions are made. Consequently, all major financial institutions have prepared — and have obtained the IRS's approval of — *master prototype plans*. These master plans (also called: Master Trusts) are umbrella arrangements for accommodating various types of employer plans, including Keoghs and SEPs.

For your "thinking things over," you should contact one or more of the major financial institutions in your business area (such as banks, mutual funds, insurance companies, etc.) Inquire about their

Keogh/SEP plans, and request literature thereon. Also request copies of their trust instrument (the qualified plan), application form, and fee schedule. Except for defined benefit plans (described below), the trustee fees are nominal: $50 to $100 per year per participant.

Basically, there are two types of tax-qualified retirement plans: (a) defined benefit, and (b) defined contribution. A defined *benefit* plan bases contributions on an actuarial formula for attaining specific dollar retirement benefits, for the participant's average compensation over his entire lifetime. The required contributions vary significantly from year to year. The amount of each year's contributions is determined from three pages of actuarial computations known as Schedule B (Form 5500). The annual fee for computing this information ranges from $1,000 to $3,000 per participant, depending on the number of participants in each plan.

Planning for specific dollar benefits at time of retirement is costly and complex. For Keoghs and SEPs, the cash outlays for defined benefit plans are far too great for struggling — and even successful — self-employment businesses. We, therefore, suggest that you disregard defined benefit plans entirely. Concentrate solely on defined *contribution* plans.

A defined contribution plan bases its contributions on a fixed and/or variable percentage of each participant's actual earnings each year. A participant's account rises or falls depending on these earnings, and on the investment performance of the trust fund manager. Defined contribution plans are of three sub-types, namely:

(1) Money purchase (pension)
(2) Profit-sharing
(3) Stock bonus

These are the kinds of options you want to look for when comparing master prototype plans for Keogh/SEP purposes.

When comparing the prototype "packages" offered by financial institutions, you want simplicity and flexibility. You want simplicity in the application form (called: *Adoption Agreement*) and in the periodic statements of plan contributions and income. You want flexibility to add and terminate employees (called: *Participant Enrollment*) and to vary the contribution percentage as business conditions (and profits) permit.

A schematic overview of your Keogh/SEP arrangement with the financial institution of your choice is presented in Figure 12.1. The

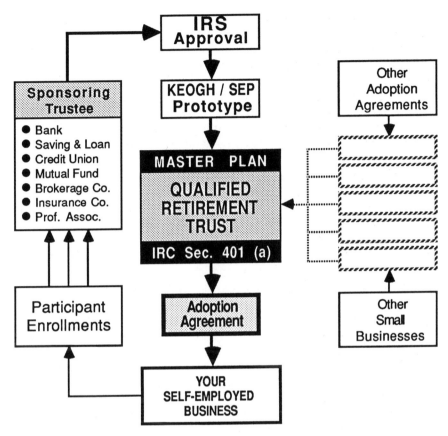

**Fig. 12.1 - Concept of Adopting Master Keogh / SEP Plan**

"bare bones" of the arrangement is a qualified retirement **trust** that meets the requirements of Section 401 of the Internal Revenue Code. For each separate plan that you acquire, make sure that the financial institution provides you with a copy of its approval letter from the IRS.

### Computing Contributory Amounts

When adopting a Keogh plan, the business owner needs to indicate what his likely percentage of contributions is going to be. He can select any percentage from 1% to 25%. Then he proceeds to compute the contributory amount for each participant based on his/her *earned income.*

The term "earned income" has a different meaning depending on whether the participant is an employee, owner-employee, or self-employed (owner-employer). Whereas, for employees and owner-employees, the "selected %" is used, for self-employeds and owner-employers a "converted %" is used. Let us explain.

In the case of a qualified employee, his earned income is the gross compensation paid to him. The contributory amount to his Keogh plan is simply the selected % times his compensation. The result is rounded to the nearest $100.

In the case of an owner-employee (person with a more than 10% interest in a partnership), determining what is earned income has a complication. If the partnership agreement calls for a "guaranteed payment" to that partner, the amount of payment is treated as employee-type compensation. For this portion, the selected % is used for contributory computations.

If, in addition to any guaranteed payment, the owner-employee also receives a prorata portion of the net profit of the business, said portion is treated as self-employment income. In this case, the selected % cannot be used. In its place, a *converted %* must be used. The converted % is lower than the selected %, as you'll see.

In the case of a self-employed individual, or owner-employer (who is self-employed), a converted % — NOT the selected % — is applied to the net profit from his business Schedule C.

The "converted %" (that which is converted from the selected %) derives from the technicalities of what constitutes earned income from self-employment. For Keogh (and also SEP) contributions, earned income is—

Net profit from Schedule C
**Less**   the "adjustment effect" when using the preprinted 92.35% on Schedule SE
**Less**   the "adjustment to income" by one-half of the SE tax

This has all been worked out into a conversion formula, namely:

$$\text{Converted } \% = \frac{\text{Selected } \%}{1 + \text{Selected } \%}$$

For example, a selected % of 15% converts to 13.043% as follows:

$$\text{Converted }\% = \frac{15\%}{1 + 15\%} = \frac{15\%}{115\%} = 13.043\%$$

Thus, while an employee's compensation would be multiplied by 15% to compute his plan contributions, a self-employed's net profit would be multiplied by 13.043% to compute his plan contributions.

Presumably, a self-employed's net profit is greater than the compensation he may pay to any one employee. If not, one has to ask: Where is the incentive for adopting any Keogh plan when there are employees involved?

## A Two-Keogh Plan

The primary advantage of a Keogh plan is that you can actually have *two* plans. One can be designated as a profit-sharing plan; the other can be designated as a pension plan. You can select any combination of contributory percentages that you want, so long as the total of the two percentages does not exceed 25%.

For example, you can adopt a profit-sharing plan with a maximum selected percentage of 15%. You can also adopt a pension plan with a maximum selected percentage of 10%. When you do this, you have to assign each plan a 3-digit number. The profit-sharing or P/S plan would be 001; the pension or PEN plan would be 002. This makes the two plans.

Having two plans adds some computational complications, but they're not too severe. They arise because you have to use two different selected %s **and** two different converted %s. To facilitate your computations in this regard, we present in Figure 12.2 a complete conversion table. Note that the conversions are given at 1% intervals. We show each conversion to three decimal places.

Having two plans provides significant contributional flexibility, whether or not employees are involved. For your P/S plan, the percentage you select (up to 15%) is totally within your discretion. It can be 0%; it can be 15%; or it can be any percentage in between. Furthermore, you can choose one percentage one year, and an entirely different percentage another year. Also, you can require a minimum of one year of service (1,000 hours) eligibility for employees, and you can put them on a 5-year or on a 3- to 7-year vesting schedule. If an employee leaves voluntarily, any unvested portion in his account is forfeited.

| Eligible Employee Selected % | Self-Employed Converted % | Eligible Employee Selected % | Self-Employed Converted % |
|---|---|---|---|
| 0 | 0.000 | 13 | 11.504 |
| 1 | 0.990 | 14 | 12.281 |
| 2 | 1.961 | 15 | 13.043 |
| 3 | 2.913 | 16 | 13.793 |
| 4 | 3.846 | 17 | 14.530 |
| 5 | 4.786 | 18 | 15.254 |
| 6 | 5.660 | 19 | 15.966 |
| 7 | 6.542 | 20 | 16.667 |
| 8 | 7.047 | 21 | 17.355 |
| 9 | 8.257 | 22 | 18.032 |
| 10 | 9.091 | 23 | 18.699 |
| 11 | 9.910 | 24 | 19.355 |
| 12 | 10.714 | 25 | 20.000 |

Fig. 12.2 - Equivalent Earned Income for Schedule C Net Profit

Your pension plan contributions are less flexible. Whatever you select as the contributory percentage, say 10%, becomes fixed. You cannot vary it within a given year, or from year to year. You must make the stated percentage contribution for each eligible employee. You must do this regardless of whether you derive a net profit from the business. Thus, a situation could arise (such as in a net loss year) where you are making contributions to your employees' Keoghs, but not to your own. To guard against this possibility, you can require that employee eligibility be two years of service. When you do this, however, each employee who completes two years of service automatically becomes 100% vested.

All Keogh plans, whether a single plan (P/S) or a combined plan (P/S + PEN), require certain tax information filings, after the contributions for each plan year have been made. For self-employed businesses, it is best that the plan year correspond with the calendar year of the owner's Form 1040. The required filing is Form 5500-C/R: *Return/Report of Employee Qualified Plan* (with fewer than 100 participants. This filing due date is on or before July 31 of each plan year.

## SEP Plans, Generally

A SEP plan — Simplified *Employee* Pension — indeed has some favorable features when a self-employed business or a partnership engages employees. The very first simplification is that whether an employer has 1, 10, or 50 employees, no annual Form 5500-C/R is required. In its place is a one-third-page form which is given to each SEP participant. This is Form 5305-SEP: Simplified Employee Pension — Individual Retirement Accounts Contribution Agreement. This is called the **employer's** SEP "Contribution Agreement."

The idea behind a SEP arrangement is that each qualified employee sets up his/her own IRA account with a financial institution of his/her own choice. To do so, the employee must subscribe to Form 5305: *Individual Retirement Trust Account.* Once the employee does this, the employer is obliged to make profit-sharing-type contributions. These contributions are limited to the lesser of $30,000 or 15% of each employee's compensation.

ALL eligible employees must set up their own individual SEP-IRA accounts. For SEP purposes, a self-employed is treated as an employee. He, too, must set up a SEP-IRA. If any qualified employee objects to setting up an IRA, the SEP arrangement is disqualified for all. Such an objection would be "good cause" for terminating that employee.

The set-up distinction between a Keogh and a SEP is depicted in Figure 12.3. The key SEP idea is that each participant — employee or employer — is on his or her own. Once a SEP contribution is made, it is 100% vested (more on the reason for this later). Each participant, via his own trustee (financial institution), can direct his investments any way he wants; can make withdrawals; can make rollovers from other IRA or other pension accounts; can make separate IRA contributions of his own (under the regular IRA rules); and can transfer his account to any approved SEP-IRA trustee at any time. Thus, the employer-contributor is totally free of any aggregate accounting for — and the safeguard of — employee funds.

An employer cannot set up a SEP plan if he currently maintains any other qualified plan. If he has a one- or two-plan Keogh in existence, for example, he has to terminate that plan. Doing so

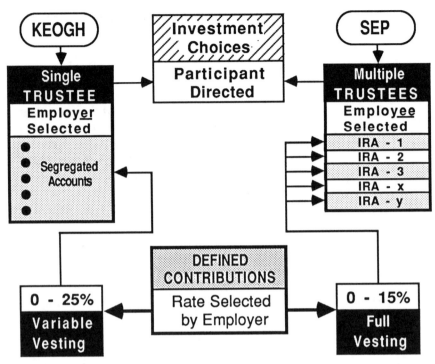

**Fig. 12.3 - Basic Distinction Between Keogh and SEP Plans**

means that he has to distribute totally all plan assets proportionately to each Keogh participant. Once this is done, he can immediately commence a SEP plan. One nice advantage of the SEP is that the distributions from a terminated Keogh can be rolled over into each participant's SEP-IRA, if he/she so chooses.

### SEP Participation Requirements

Whether an employer establishes a Keogh or SEP plan, the age requirement for participation is the same: at least 21 years old. From this point on, the participation requirements differ.

Perhaps the greatest single difference between a Keogh and a SEP is the service requirement. For SEPs, eligibility for participation applies to each employee who—

*Has performed service for the employer during at least 3 of the immediately preceding 5 years.* [IRC Sec. 408(k)(2)(B)]

Here, the term "service" means — *any work performed for any period of time, however short.* In other words, one **hour** or more in any referenced year.

This service requirement of at least three years applies also to employers. In other words, as a newly self-employed individual, you cannot set up your own SEP-IRA, make immediate contributions to it, and deny eligibility to your employees until each has worked for you three years. If you start a SEP plan the day after you start your business, the eligibility requirement for your employees is one day: NOT three years. This is one reason why, in the early part of this chapter, we suggested waiting three years before deciding on any Keogh or SEP plan. Once you have waited three years before contributing to your own SEP-IRA, you can require others also to wait three years.

Once an employee has met the 3-year service requirement, any contribution you make to his SEP-IRA is immediately 100% vested. The tax code section on point [Sec. 408(k)(4)] states it this way:

> A [SEP] *meets the requirements of* [a qualified trust] *only if*—
> *(A) employer contributions thereto are not conditioned on the retention in such pension of any portion of the amount contributed, and*
> *(B) there is no prohibition imposed by the employer on withdrawals from the* [SEP].

This makes it pretty clear. Once you contribute to an employee's SEP-IRA, you have no further strings on that money. You do, however, get a business expense deduction on your Schedule C (or on Schedule F or on your partnership return) for all employee contributions made.

Under separate provisions of the tax code, you can exclude the following employees (regardless of years of service):

A. Those covered by collective bargaining (labor union) agreements, and
B. Those whose total compensation for the year is less than $350.

## SEP Uniformity

Subsection 408(k)(3)(C) is titled: Contributions Must Bear Uniform Relationship to Total Compensation. The "uniform relationship" must relate to compensation: **not** to years of service. This is to avoid favoring the owner and those employees who may have been with him since the business started.

The SEP uniformity concept means that, if an employer sets the maximum 15% as his contribution percentage, he has to apply this same percentage across the board to all employee participants. Statutorily, this uniformity requirement *ceases* for those compensations in excess of $200,000. It is doubtful that any self-employed business owners pay their employees in excess of this amount. This tells us that SEP plans may be used by many other forms of business.

For self-employeds, the uniformity rule has another feature of interest. This is stated in Regulation 1.408-8(c)(1), to wit—

*A rate of contribution which decreases as compensation increases shall be considered uniform.*

Interpreted, this SEP rule means that an employer can decrease his percentage of contribution as the compensation of his employees increases. For example, he may set 15% contribution for employees earning $20,000 or less; 10% for those earning from $20,000 up to $35,000; and 5% for those earning over $35,000.

Within the context of this uniform relationship requirement, the specific contributory percentage is entirely within the discretion of the employer. He may vary it from year to year, if he so chooses. Whether he varies the rate of contribution or not, he must notify each employee of his *allocation formula*, and show each employer how that employee's contribution amount is computed. Usually, this is done in January of each year, when the employer is preparing Forms W-2 for all employees. The specific contribution amount is entered in one of the boxes labeled: **Other**, on the W-2.

The SEP contribution amount is **not** included in the employee's gross compensation, nor is it given to the employee in cash. It must be forwarded directly to the employee's IRA trustee. Once deposited in the employee's SEP-IRA trust account, it is nonrecoverable by the employer. The "mechanics" of SEP contributions are portrayed in Figure 12.4.

What about the employer's own SEP-IRA? What rate of contributions does he make?

Answer: The employer has to follow the same uniformity rule he applies to his employees. There is just one difference. He has to use the *converted* percentages shown in Figure 12.2 for Keogh

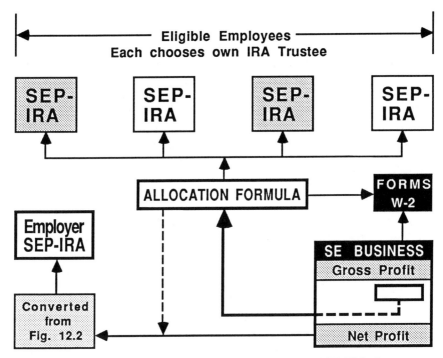

**Fig. 12.4 - The Mechanics of Contributions to SEP-IRA Accounts**

plans. Thus, the maximum rate of contribution to his own SEP is 13.043%. This corresponds to the maximum 15% he can contribute to his employees.

## Keogh and SEP Compared

There are similarities and differences between Keoghs and SEPs. Let us compare the two, from your point of view as a self-employed business owner.

As to the age for eligibility requirement, there are no differences. Every participant must be at least 21 years old. Very few persons start self-employment at this early age. More often than not, self-employeds are in the "forty plus" age category.

As to the deductibility of your retirement contributions on Form 1040 (as adjustments to total income), there are no differences either. The contributory amounts may differ, but their deductibility is the same. The specific adjustment line on Form 1040 reads—

*Keogh retirement plan and self-employed SEP deduction.*

Unfortunately, this identification line implies that you can have a Keogh and a SEP simultaneously. You can not. While in a given year, you may indeed have both types of plans, you cannot have them simultaneously. You must terminate one before starting the other. This means that you will have a "short year" for each plan. Your earned income, on which you base your contributions, must correspond proportionately to each short year. The Keogh and SEP short years must be distinct and separate from each other, with no overlapping.

In a qualifying year in which you have no employees whatsoever, a Keogh plan permits a substantially higher contribution than does a SEP. Using Figure 12.2, your maximum Keogh contribution would be 20%, compared with a maximum SEP contribution of 13%. On a net earnings of $100,000 for example, $7,000 more could be contributed to a Keogh than to a SEP. Over the years to your retirement, this difference, compounded, could mean quite a difference.

Thus, the real focus for decision-making between Keogh and SEP is the matter of employees. If they meet the years of service requirements, you MUST include them in your plan. You cannot "lease" employees from other companies, or set up a subsidiary "service" company of your own, to avoid employee Keogh/SEP participations. Nor can you engage in a "pattern of avoidance" by routinely terminating employees just as they become eligible for participation. Large corporations may do these things and get away with them, but not you as a small entrepreneur.

Once you engage one or more employees on an ongoing basis, there is only one delay-type strategy that you can use. This is the statutory years-of-service requirement. For Keogh, you have two options: one year's service with variable vesting, or two years' service with 100% vesting. For Keogh, a year of service is 1,000 hours or more. With SEP, you have only one option: three years of service with 100% vesting. For SEP, a year of service is one hour or more.

Most small businesses experience high rates of employee turnover. Employees use the opportunity to gain experience, then move on elsewhere. If the nature of your business is such that high turnover is the norm, a 2-year-eligibility Keogh could be quite beneficial for your own contributions. If the nature of your business is such that you want to build up a small, permanent staff, a 1-year eligibility Keogh with variable vesting (3, 5, 7 years) could be advantageous. Much depends on the number of employees you expect to max out at, throughout your business life. As a practical limit, we recommend Keoghs only up to 10 participants.

On the other hand, if the nature of your business is such that you must engage more than 10 employees in any given year, SEPs are definitely more practical. A SEP permits you to set a 3-year eligibility requirement before making contributions to your employees' IRA accounts. In the meantime, you get a 3-year "jump start" in your own SEP-IRA (assuming you waited three years after starting you business before starting any retirement plan). Also, in a 3-year eligibility period, there could be any number of voluntary terminations to further jump-start your own contributions, in comparison with those you are obliged to make for your employees.

If, after three years after starting your business, you decide on a Keogh or SEP, your decision is not cast in concrete. You can terminate one and start the other, as conditions dictate. It is not uncommon for self-employed owners to adopt a Keogh for a few years, terminate it, adopt a SEP for a few years, terminate that, adopt another Keogh . . . and so on.

## After Age 59-1/2

There is one particular advantage that self-employed individuals have over their employees. Come age 59-1/2 and beyond, most self-employeds are still in business. Other persons who are not self-employed are not readily employable after 59-1/2.

Why age 59-1/2?

Three reasons, actually. This is the age after which no tax penalties apply for withdrawals from a Keogh or SEP. Each is a tax-deferred retirement plan. Any withdrawal prior to age 59-1/2 is subject to a 10% federal *excise* tax, in addition to regular tax.

The second reason is that this is the age that many employees start thinking about their own retirement. Prompting them in this regard is their eye on collecting their Social Security benefits which start at age 62. Access to Keogh/SEP money becomes highly attractive for "integrated" Social Security/Keogh/SEP retirement plans. Enticing such employees into retirement is not difficult to do.

A third reason is that, at over age 59-1/2, a self-employed owner can downsize his business substantially . . . with clear conscience. Having employees becomes no longer a social or political responsibility. He can sell off or abandon parts of the business, and keep the core expertise and core customer base for himself. He can convert to a one-man (or she to a one-woman) business with NO EMPLOYEES. He/she can then set up a maximum contributory Keogh, and "pack in" tax deductible contributions at the rate of 20% until age 70-1/2. This provides a good 10-year span of time for a single-participant Keogh. Concurrently, at age 70, he/she becomes eligible to commence receiving maximum possible Social Security benefits.

By April 1 of the year following the year you attain age 70-1/2, distributions from your Keogh and SEP plans become mandatory. You must terminate each plan and arrange to take the money. If a Keogh, you can take it out in a lump-sum and get favorable tax treatment called: *special averaging* (if born before 1936). If a SEP, you don't get the special-averaging treatment. Either plan can be terminated by converting it to an immediate annuity which pays out uniformly in 10 or more years.

What is to stop you from continuing self-employment after age 70-1/2?

Nothing, really . . . if your health is good. Even if you don't need the money, you can continue.

If you do continue, you can re-ignite the employee routine over again. This time, however, employ your adult children, your grandchildren, your grandnephews and your grandnieces. Pay them the maximum appropriate wages that you can. Set up a SEP-IRA for each family member and contribute at the maximum rate. Deliberately drive your own net earnings down to zero. This way, you won't pay any additional income tax or any self-employment tax.

If you program things right, continuing self-employment after age 70-1/2 can become your perpetual family-in-motion machine. The financial security and independence that you'll experience will be truly exciting. This, then, becomes your ultimate reward for being self-employed.

# ABOUT
# THE AUTHOR

---

Holmes F. Crouch

---

Born on a small farm in southern Maryland, Holmes was graduated from the U.S. Coast Guard Academy with a Bachelor's Degree in Marine Engineering. While serving on active duty, he wrote many technical articles on maritime matters. After attaining the rank of Lieutenant Commander, he resigned to pursue a career as a nuclear engineer.

Continuing his education, he earned a Master's Degree in Nuclear Engineering from the University of California. He also authored two books on nuclear propulsion. As a result of the tax write-offs associated with writing these books, the IRS audited his returns. The IRS's handling of the audit procedure so annoyed Holmes that he undertook to become as knowledgeable as possible regarding tax procedures. He became a licensed private Tax Practitioner by passing an examination administered by the IRS. Having attained this credential, he started his own tax preparation and counseling business in 1972.

In the early years of his tax practice, he was a regular talk-show guest on San Francisco's KGO Radio responding to hundreds of phone-in tax questions from listeners. He was a much sought-after guest speaker at many business seminars and taxpayer meetings. He also provided counseling on special tax problems, such as divorce matters, property exchanges, timber harvesting, mining ventures, animal breeding, independent contractors, selling businesses, and offices-at-home. Over the past 20 years, he has prepared nearly 9,000 tax returns for individuals, estates, and small businesses.

During the tax season of January through April, he prepares returns in a unique manner. During a single meeting, he completes the return . . . *on the spot!* The client leaves with his return signed, sealed, and in a stamped envelope. His unique approach to preparing returns and his personal interest in his clients' tax affairs have honed his professional proficiency. His expertise extends through itemized deductions, computer-matching of income sources, capital gains and losses, business expenses and cost of goods, residential rental expenses, limited and general partnership activities, closely-held corporations, to family farms and ranches.

He remembers spending 12 straight hours completing a doctor's complex return. The next year, the doctor, having moved away, utilized a large accounting firm to prepare his return. Their accountant was so impressed by the manner in which the prior return was prepared that he recommended the doctor travel the 500 miles each year to have Holmes continue doing it.

He recalls preparing a return for an unemployed welder, for which he charged no fee. Two years later the welder came back and had his return prepared. He paid the regular fee . . . and then added a $300 tip.

During the off season, he represents clients at IRS audits and appeals. In one case a shoe salesman's audit was scheduled to last three hours. However, after examining Holmes' documentation it was concluded in 15 minutes with "no change" to his return. In another instance he went to an audit of a custom jeweler that the IRS dragged out for more than six hours. But, supported by Holmes' documentation, the client's return was accepted by the IRS with "no change."

Then there was the audit of a language translator that lasted two full days. The auditor scrutinized more than $1.25 million in gross receipts, all direct costs, and operating expenses. Even though all expensed items were documented and verified, the auditor decided that more than $23,000 of expenses ought to be listed as capital items for depreciation instead. If this had been enforced it would have resulted in a significant additional amount of tax. Holmes strongly disagreed and after many hours explanation got the amount reduced by more than 60% on behalf of his client.

He has dealt extensively with gift, death and trust tax returns. These preparations have involved him in the tax aspects of wills, estate planning, trustee duties, probate, marital and charitable bequests, gift and death exemptions, and property titling.

Although not an attorney, he prepares Petitions to the U.S. Tax Court for clients. He details the IRS errors and taxpayer facts by citing pertinent sections of tax law and regulations. In a recent case involving an attorney's ex-spouse, the IRS asserted a tax deficiency of $155,000. On behalf of his client, he petitioned the Tax Court and within six months the IRS conceded the case.

*Over the years, Holmes has observed that the IRS is not the industrious, impartial, and competent federal agency that its official public imaging would have us believe.*

He found that, at times, under the slightest pretext, the IRS has interpreted against a taxpayer in order to assess maximum penalties, and may even delay pending matters so as to increase interest due on additional taxes. He has confronted the IRS in his own behalf on five separate occasions, going before the U.S. Claims Court, U.S. District Court, and U.S. Tax Court. These were court actions that tested specific sections of the Internal Revenue Code which he found ambiguous, inequitable, and abusively interpreted by the IRS.

Disturbed by the conduct of the IRS and by the general lack of tax knowledge by most individuals, he began an innovative series of taxpayer-oriented Federal tax guides. To fulfill this need, he undertook the writing of a series of guidebooks that provide in-depth knowledge on one tax subject at a time. He focuses on subjects that plague taxpayers all throughout the year. Hence, his formulation of the "Allyear" Tax Guides. This book is one in the series. Several have already been completed (see listing on next page) and others are in process.

The author is indebted to his wife, Irma Jean, and daughter, Barbara MacRae, for the word processing and computer graphics that turn his experiences into the reality of these publications. Holmes welcomes comments, questions, and suggestions from his readers. He can be contacted through the publisher.

# ALLYEAR
## TAX GUIDES IN PRINT

**Series 100 - INDIVIDUALS AND FAMILIES**

101 - Tax Guide: BEING SELF-EMPLOYED
102 - Tax Guide: BUSINESS AUTO & TRAVEL
104 - Tax Guide: RESOLVING DIVORCE ISSUES

**Series 200 - INVESTORS AND BUSINESSES**

201 - Tax Guide: INVESTOR GAINS & LOSSES
203 - Tax Guide: STARTING YOUR BUSINESS

**Series 300 - RETIREES AND ESTATES**

303 - Tax Guide: WRITING YOUR WILL
304 - Tax Guide: YOUR EXECUTOR DUTIES

**Series 400 - OWNERS AND SELLERS**

401 - Tax Guide: RENTAL REAL ESTATE
403 - Tax Guide: SELLING YOUR HOME

**Series 500 - AUDITS AND APPEALS**

502 - Tax Guide: WINNING YOUR AUDIT
503 - Tax Guide: DISAGREEING WITH THE IRS
504 - Tax Guide: GOING INTO TAX COURT

To obtain any of the above 12 books,
contact your local bookstore or bookseller.

Otherwise, phone or write to:

**Allyear Tax Guides**
**20484 Glen Brae Dr.**
**Saratoga, CA   95070**

**Phone:     (408) 867-2628**